FOR MUM AND DAD

British Library Cataloguing in Publication Data

Pike, Mary Ann
  Town and country fare and fable.
  1. Cookery, British   2. Great Britain – Social
  life and customs – 20th century
  I. Title
  641.5'941   TX717
  ISBN 0–7153–7720–5

Library of Congress Catalog Card Number 78-60989

Printed in Great Britain
by A. Wheaton & Co Limited, Exeter
for David & Charles (Publishers) Limited
Brunel House   Newton Abbot   Devon

Published in the United States of America
by David & Charles Inc
North Pomfret   Vermont 05053   USA

Published in Canada
by Douglas David & Charles Limited
1875 Welch Street   North Vancouver   BC

Contents

Introduction

This work started out as an article that simply grew and grew until it was no longer an article but a book. Indeed it is not finished yet – I doubt if it ever will be as fresh material comes to light all the time – but I had to draw a line somewhere.

I have striven to include newly-born culinary offerings as well as to preserve many regional recipes and customs which are in danger of sinking into oblivion. It is curious that, in some places, people are quite unaware of their local recipes while, in other places, they nurture them with pride. For instance, Coventry's godcakes have been practically abandoned, while Eccles cakes have become world famous specialities, and yet they are both pastry and currant mixtures.

My recipes have been both donated and culled from here, there and everywhere. My thanks go to the large number of correspondents who have passed on local information so generously.

I have tried to tailor the recipes into some sort of conformity so that the amounts are suitable for today's smaller families. No cook would thank me for getting her to bake a cake to feed the whole street – and the original 'receipt' for a Bury simnel would do just that! I have also given the approximate number of servings where possible. However I must stress that these are only guidelines. What one person calls a slap-up meal, another regards as a mere snack! For example, in my travels for this book, I discovered that people in the north generally eat far more heartily than southerners.

The first four sections of the book are concerned with recipes for which England, Wales, Scotland and Ireland are famous. The recipes which follow these sections are listed under the regional name – county, town, village or field (eg Honiton Fairings) – by which they are most commonly known. All these places are listed alphabetically. I hope that this method will enable readers unfamiliar with the British Isles to easily locate the recipe they require.

This is no book for teaching people to cook – there are enough volumes on pastry-making and egg-scrambling – but rather a culinary patchwork of fare and fable which I hope will entertain all those tempted to delve into its pages.

Mary Ann Pike
Prittlewell 1978

ENGLAND

Beef

> Oh! The roast beef of England,
> And old England's roast beef.

So penned Henry Fielding (1707–54) in his *Grub Street Opera*. And Nathaniel Hawthorne (1804–64) noted 'Dr. Johnson's morality was as English an article as a beefsteak' in *Our Old House*. Beef has certainly enjoyed a prominent position in English fare from very early times. The Roman soldiers favoured English beef because it was so full of flavour in comparison with beef from the cattle they had attempted to raise in their Mediterranean settlements, where the grazing was not so lush.

Throughout the ages, beef has been salted and brined, and stored in barrels to feed sailors at sea, and to sustain citizens in towns under siege. In chronicles of culinary affairs, beef is recorded as having graced the elaborate feasting tables of the wealthy in both medieval and Tudor times, and visiting foreign noblemen were always suitably impressed with the extravagant size of the joints and their supreme succulence. A 'receipt' of the fifteenth century describes how thick steaks of beef were browned, sprinkled with cinnamon spice and served with some sharp sauce.

In Victorian days the joints of beef were still very large, by today's standards, and a 24lb joint of rib beef was a normal Sunday roast. It is no fallacy that the larger the joint, the better its flavour, but such a surplus of roast meat eventually inspired, perhaps as families became smaller, the old jingle:

> Hot on Sunday,
> Cold on Monday,
> Hashed on Tuesday,
> Minced on Wednesday,
> Curried on Thursday,
> Broth on Friday,
> Cottage Pie Saturday.

The beef now eaten in England comes from many different herds scattered all over the country, with Hereford cattle reigning as perhaps the choicest; from Scotland, where the Aberdeen Angus is unsurpassed; and, sad to say, from imported animals. As a very general guide, joints of beef such as sirloin, topside and aitchbone, should be roasted for 20min per lb, plus an additional 20min. They should be basted frequently, from dripping added to the meat tin if the meat is without much fat. It is appropriate to record here that cattle are bred much leaner these days than fifty or so years ago, as apparently the English housewife dislikes purchasing fatty beef. This has resulted in some pretty tasteless meat.

Traditionally roast beef is served with roast potatoes, Yorkshire pudding, 'two veg', and horse-radish sauce. The root for the latter should be dug under a full moon as, according to old lore, its flavour is more pungent then. Some people like mustard better, but in our household this is reserved for beefsteaks.

> A woman, a steak, and a walnut tree,
> More you beat 'em, better they be.

Bubble and Squeak is a firm old English favourite and is really a method of using leftover vegetables. However, odd bits of meat can be added too. The variations are endless and this recipe is just a guide.

Bubble and Squeak

1lb (450g) leftover cabbage, boiled
1lb (450g) leftover potatoes (mashed or boiled)
Few slices cold roast beef or whatever
Salt and pepper
Dripping

Chop the cabbage, potatoes (if not already mashed) and beef. Mix together and season well. Melt some dripping in a frying pan and add the chopped mixture. Stir it around to brown all over. When well heated through, turn onto hot plates and serve immediately. The name supposedly originated due to the sound of 'bubbling and squeaking' in the pan.

7

Toad-in-the-hole is a batter dish made with Yorkshire pudding poured these days over sausages, or occasionally lamb chops. However years ago, it was a much more extravagant dish with steak, kidneys, oysters and mushrooms submerged in the batter.

Toad-in-the-Hole   (Serves 4)

Yorkshire pudding (see under *Yorkshire*) *made from 4oz*
  (112g) plain flour, pinch salt, 2 eggs and ½ pint (280ml)
  milk
4 fat sausages
4oz (112g) mushrooms
2 kidneys sliced
Dripping or lard
Salt and pepper

Make the Yorkshire batter pudding and leave to stand. Grease a meat tin with dripping and lay the sausages in it. Add the mushrooms, which should be washed but not sliced, and the kidneys. Season well and pour in the batter. Bake for about an hour at 400°F (200°C/Gas mark 6). Cut into slabs and serve with vegetables and thick gravy.

Bacon and Eggs

> 'No business before breakfast, Glum' says the King.
> 'Breakfast first, business next'.
>   (W. M. Thackeray, 1811–63 in *The Rose and the Ring*)

The English have always been renowned for their breakfasts, but whatever lavish breakfasts were gorged in yesteryear, bacon and eggs is now considered the traditional English breakfast. It is I feel a dish which must be cooked to one's own taste. Some like their bacon half raw, others like it brown and crumbly; some like eggs with runny yolks, others like them rock hard; some like their egg whites smooth and white, others like them frilly round the edges. So take one frying pan and do your own thing! On Sundays, when we go mad, we sometimes gorge on mushrooms, tomatoes and fried bread too. I must mention also the rinds which are cut off the rashers and fried in little curls.

At the other end of the day, fish and chips make a traditional English supper, although lots of people also eat them for lunch. Chips were most probably introduced to Britain by a Belgian man who first sold them on a market stall in the 1860s in Dundee (served with boiled peas), and many reports claim that they were married to fried fish in Lancashire some decades later. There are surprisingly few recipes for fish and chips in English cookery books for the simple reason that most people buy this meal, when there is no time to cook anything else, at their local frying joint. But fish and chips are quite easy to cook at home and many different fish can be sampled.

Fish 'n' Chips

Allow 2 fillets of plaice or 1 whole fish (or cod, rock salmon, etc) and about 8oz (225g) potatoes for each person. Peel the potatoes, cut into chips, and wrap them in a clean cloth to get them as dry as possible. (Some people like to soak them in cold water for about an hour before drying them, but I do not think it makes much difference.) Make a coating batter from 4oz (112g) flour, pinch of salt, 1 beaten egg, and about ¼ pint (140ml) of milk. Leave to stand for a minute or so. Wash the fish and pat dry. Heat some oil in a deep frying pan to about 360°F (182°C) or until 1in cube of bread browns in 1min. Dip the fish in the batter and drop into the hot oil. Do not fry more than a couple of pieces of fish at once otherwise the oil will become too cool and the batter will be soggy. Fry until golden brown – about 5–10min. Scoop out, shaking off excess oil, and keep warm while you fry the other pieces. Make up more batter if required.

Finally deep fry the chips, in batches if necessary, and preferably with the aid of a chip basket. It is generally considered best to fry them twice – once for 6–7min, and then again for a couple of minutes just before putting them on the plates to get them really crisp. Basic condiments for fish and chips, especially in newspaper, are salt and vinegar, whereas more elegant accompaniments on posh occasions can include lemon wedges and tartare sauce.

Tea

Perhaps the most famous English culinary institution is tea, although of course most of it does come from the Far East. According to oriental mythology, Ta-Mo, a Buddhist missionary in China in the sixth century vowed, in order to demonstrate an example of devoutness, to remain awake until his missionary work was finished – a period of taxing duration. One day, however, he was overcome by sleep, and allowed his eyes to shut. On waking, he was so ashamed of his infidelity that he pulled his eyelids off and threw them to the ground. Buddha, so the tale goes, caused the eyelashes to root and grow into a remarkable plant of eternal wakefulness. (Tea, of course, is a stimulant and contains caffeine.)

When tea was first introduced into England, possibly by the Dutch sometime in the early seventeenth century, it fetched anything up to £14 per lb – an astronomical price in those days. This explains why many antique tea caddies are lockable. However, when the East India Company's monopoly with China ceased, the cost of tea fell to more acceptable levels.

Before the arrival of tea in England, coffee had been the country's national drink. The first public advertisement for tea appeared in *The London Gazette* in 1658. It read: 'That excellent and by all Physicians approved drink, called Chinese Tcha, by other nations Tay, alias Tea, is sold at Sultaness Cophee House, Sweetin's Rents, Royal Exchange, London'. Tea was served in Garraway's Coffee House, in Exchange Alley, London, in 1660. The beverage soon became very popular, but not with Jonas Hanway, who wrote in a letter condemning tea, 'Chambermaids have lost their bloom by sipping tea'. Gladstone, however, was very partial to tea. He even took a hot water bottle filled with tea to bed with him – to keep his toes warm, and his thirst quenched.

Some early English tea drinkers flavoured, or eked out (?), their tea with saffron, or peach leaves. The addition of milk and sugar came into vogue in time, but it is a habit peculiar to the British Isles. Of the other two great tea drinking nations, the Chinese prefer their tea black or scented, and the Russians stir jam into their cuppas.

As well as numerous fortune-telling possibilities there is much folklore connected with tea. For instance, legend says that you should never stir tea in the pot or you will provoke a family quarrel, and if two women both pour tea from the same pot, one of them will shortly become pregnant!

The English afternoon teatime is said to have been invented by Anne, Duchess of Bedford (1788–1861) who complained of a 'sinking feeling' in the afternoon and succeeded in dispelling it with tea and cakes. The acquaintances of the Duchess joined her little snacks, and soon took to having teatime revivals themselves.

WALES

Leeks

The Welsh must surely have more claims on the leek than any other race. Being the country's national emblem – along with the daffodil – patriots always choose a leek dish on St David's Day, 1 March, and many still sport a leek in their hats. The origin of the latter custom is explained in many legends. One old tale suggests that the Welsh took to wearing leeks after they had successfully conquered some Saxon invaders. Another legend, popularised by Shakespeare in his play *King Henry the Fifth*, tells of Welsh soldiers putting leeks in their Monmouth caps so as to distinguish themselves from the enemy. This practice could not have been very successful as the battle for which the plan was adopted, that of Crécy in 1346, was fought in a field of leeks! A third explanation for the Welshman's association with the leek is blamed on St David, who apparently survived on a leek diet throughout the Lenten fast.

An unusual custom was traditionally observed in the mess room of the Welsh Guards on St David's Day. After dinner, a tray of leeks was ceremoniously carried round the table, and any soldier new to the regiment had to take one. Then, posed precariously with one foot on the table and the other on his chair, he had to eat it, accompanied by the roll of drums. The newcomer was then officially recognised as a true Welshman.

Another Welsh custom concerning leeks was observed by many a young maiden at Hallowe'en. The girl had to walk backwards into the garden and stick a knife in the bed of leeks. According to tradition, she could then expect to see a vision of her future husband.

Leeks of course feature prominently in the Welsh kitchen (see Anglesey section) and are always included, when in season, in Welsh Cawl – Cawl Cymreig. This is a thick soup, now generally made with mutton, but originally, since no farmer would consider allocating one of his prize lambs for the soup pot, it was made with a much cheaper cut like kid or bacon. An old Welsh proverb, attributed to Cattwg the Wise claims, 'It is as good to drink the broth as to eat the meat'. And certainly, this cawl does make a substantial meal. Ideally, the cawl should be made one day in advance so that the fat can be skimmed off when it is cold, otherwise it tastes too thick and is not so pleasant to eat.

Welsh Cawl or Cawl Cymreig

2lb (900g) scrag end lamb (approx)
Few chopped bacon rinds
2 large onions, skinned and sliced
2 or 3 carrots, scraped and chopped
3 leeks, scraped and chopped
2 small turnips, scraped and chopped
Little pepper
Good pinch of salt
1tsp dried herbs
2oz (56g) pearl barley
Chopped parsley (optional)
Water to cover

Trim the lamb of any excess fat. Put in a stew pan with the chopped bacon rinds, onions, carrots, leeks and turnips. (Actually, more or less any vegetable can be included – even potatoes in some recipes.) Season with pepper. Add salt and dried herbs. Cover with water and bring to the boil. Spoon off any scum. Cover and simmer for 2–3hr, depending on the meat. Strain into a bowl. Cut the meat away from the bones, which are now discarded, and add with the vegetables to the stock. Leave overnight and next day skim off the layer of fat. Add the pearl barley and reheat thoroughly, until the barley is cooked. Add the chopped parsley just before serving.

Traditionally, this piping-hot soup was served up in little wooden cawl bowls and supped from wooden spoons – hand carved by local craftsmen – so that it did not burn the mouth.

Another vegetable sometimes put in the cawl is laver. This edible variety of seaweed is found around the Welsh coast, especially in the south. Gathered in its natural state, laver must be thoroughly washed to remove all traces of grit, and boiled in seawater for 6hr, before it is tender enough for consumption. Commercially, it is then minced and left overnight before becoming laverbread – a somewhat confusing name as it is not a bread at all, but similar to a spinach purée. One explanation of the name is believed to be the old custom of frying laver for breakfast and skilfully twisting it with a knife to resemble a French roll. In Wales, laverbread is sold in the prepared state in the markets, such as Swansea, where women will coax you to buy from their large bowls of the dark greeny speciality. Years ago, those wishing to pick laver from the rocks had to pay a £1 fee, to the landowner, for the privilege. Now anyone with enough knowledge of what to pick from the array of sea foliage can go laver-hunting freely.

Laver is an 'acquired taste', but one should perhaps persevere and learn to like the seaweed as it is claimed to be an excellent health food, containing some fifty-two minerals. The Welsh make it into a sauce to accompany lamb.

Welsh Laver Sauce

1lb (450g) laverbread
Juice of 1 Seville orange
3oz (84g) butter
Gravy from the roasted joint
Salt and pepper

Mix all the ingredients together and heat until simmering. Pour over roasted lamb and serve.

Laverbread is also made into little cakes which are fried and served with gammon, or bacon, and eggs.

Welsh Laverbread Cakes

1lb (450g) laverbread
Fine oatmeal
Bacon fat

Mix the laverbread with sufficient oatmeal so that little flat cakes can be moulded. Fry in hot bacon fat for about 5min on each side. Drain off excess fat and serve with fried gammon and eggs.

Welsh Lamb

England has her roast beef and Wales has her roast lamb; the latter, in an uncooked state, cavort on every available hillside in Wales. As well as laver sauce, the Welsh like ordinary mint sauce on their roast lamb, and sometimes, for a change, they baste a joint with a mixture of honey and cider during the cooking. This results in an interesting and rather unusual flavour.

Still on the subject of lamb, there is a recipe for little mutton pies, or katt pies as they were sometimes called. These were traditional fare at the old 'Mop' or hiring fairs which were held in November.

Welsh Mutton Pies or Katt Pies

PASTRY
8oz (225g) shredded suet
¾ cup boiling water
1lb (450g) flour
Good pinch of salt
FILLING
12oz (337g) minced lamb
8oz (225g) currants
8oz (225g) brown sugar
Salt and pepper
Milk for glazing

Boil the shredded suet in the water for about 5min. Remove from heat and add the flour and salt rapidly. Stir until the mixture leaves the sides of the pan clean and turn onto a board, well dusted with flour. As soon as it is cool enough to handle, roll out to about ⅜in thick and line as many greased patty tins – or en cocotte dishes if preferred – as possible with two-thirds of the pastry. Spoon alternate layers of lamb, currants, and sugar into the pastry cases and season as liked. Roll remaining pastry out and cut lids. Place on the pies and brush with milk. Bake in an oven preheated to 375°F (190°C; Gas mark 5) for anything from 25 to 40min depending on the size of the pies. The recipe can also be made using one large pie dish.

Welshmen have always been partial to a bit of toasted cheese. There is a rather delightful tale, attributed to the eminent sixteenth-century physician Andrew Boorde – who started his career by being admitted as a member of the Carthusian order. In 1529, however, he was released from his monastic vows as he confessed he was unable to endure the 'rugosyte off your relygyon'. Boorde became an author and was famed for his volumes on diet and health cookery such as *Compendyous Regyment or A Dyetary of Health*. His tale about Welshmen in heaven was brought to my notice by Sheila Hutchins in her *Your Granny's Cookbook* (Daily Express Publications). The story describes how a number of Welshmen were chattering endlessly up in heaven. St Peter became tired of the noise and so devised a plan to get rid of the chatterboxes. Craftily, he ran outside the gates of heaven and shouted, 'Toasted cheese, toasted cheese', and the Welshmen were fooled into thinking that toasted cheese was cooking just outside the gates. Once the hungry Welshmen had all run outside, St Peter slammed the gates of heaven, locking them out. That, so Boorde explained, is why there are no Welshmen in heaven!

The Welsh Rarebit or Rabbit theme has travelled far and wide. Even a Scot, Robert Louis Stevenson in the person of Ben Gunn confessed, 'Many's the long night I've dreamed of cheese – toasted, mostly' (*Treasure Island*). There are numerous recipes varying from dry cheese plonked on bread and shoved under the grill, to complicated toppings with a dozen ingredients. Every recipe is claimed by its devotees to be the real Welsh thing. The following versions are two of the most popular.

Welsh Rarebit – Caws Pobi (1)

8oz (225g) strong Cheddar cheese
1tsp dry mustard
Good shake of freshly ground pepper
1tbsp Worcestershire sauce
3tbsp beer
Buttered toast

Grate the cheese into a saucepan. Add the mustard, pepper, sauce and beer. Stir over a low heat until the mixture is thick and smooth. Pour over buttered toast and sizzle it under the grill.

Welsh Rarebit – Caws Pobi (2)

4 large onions
Salt and pepper
Butter
6 slices of strong cheese
6 slices of buttered toast

Wash, peel and slice the onions. Season and fry gently in butter until soft and transparent. Divide roughly into 2 portions and arrange 1 on the slices of buttered toast. Lay a slice of cheese on top of the onions, and pile the second lot of onions on top of the cheese. Put under a hot grill until the cheese oozes, beautifully melted.

As with other Celtic races, the bakestone or griddle was much favoured in the Welsh kitchen. This was basically a huge round of metal about an inch thick, heated over an open fire. These little Welsh cakes were always cooked on a bakestone but a lightly greased heavy-based frying pan will suffice.

Welsh Cakes – Pice ar y Maen

4oz (112g) butter
4oz (112g) lard
1lb (450g) self-raising flour
Pinch of salt
4oz (112g) sugar
6oz (168g) currants
1 egg, beaten
Milk to mix

Rub the butter and lard into the flour and salt until the mixture resembles breadcrumbs. Stir in the sugar and currants. Add the egg and sufficient milk to make a stiff paste. Turn the dough onto a floured board and knead until smooth and free from any cracks. Roll out and cut 3in rounds with a cutter or glass. Heat the greased griddle or frying pan and cook the cakes on each side, until golden brown, in batches. They are best eaten whilst still hot, split and buttered.

SCOTLAND

'Oats,' wrote Samuel Johnson, in his *Dictionary of the English Language*, 'A grain, which in England is generally given to horses, but in Scotland supports the people'. Indeed, the Scottish people, especially the poorer working classes, did once rely very much on oatmeal for their survival. However, even with more prosperity and a generally better standard of living, oatmeal has not been cast completely out of the Scottish kitchen. Far from it. Many oatmeal recipes are still enthusiastically prepared today. Surprisingly, oatmeal varies considerably from area to area, and knowledgeable folk make as much fuss about the differences as do wine connoisseurs with their grapes. Midlothian oatmeal is considered by many experts to be unsurpassable.

The commonest recipe using oatmeal is of course that for the breakfast filler – porridge, or 'the halesome parritch, chief o' Scotia's food' as Robert Burns described it. In old Scottish kitchens a cast iron Carron goblet, made at the Carron foundry in Falkirk, was invariably kept solely for porridge making, and a wooden stick called a spurtle, theevil or gruel-tree, according to the region you were in, was used for stirring. This is the traditional porridge recipe.

Porridge

For each person:
1 breakfast cup water
1¼oz (35g) good quality oatmeal
½tsp salt

Bring water to boil in a pan. Take the oatmeal in one hand and trickle it into the water, stirring continuously (clockwise for luck!) with a porridge stick in your other hand. Put lid on pan and cook for 10min. Remove lid, add salt, replace lid and continue to cook for another 10–20min, according to the type of oatmeal used. Incidentally, never put the salt in the water in the first instance as it hardens the oatmeal and prevents it from swelling fully. Ladle into cold porringers, or bowls, and serve with a separate bowl of cream or cold milk. The steaming hot porridge is traditionally eaten with horn spoons, and dipped in the cold cream or milk so that one does not burn one's mouth.

> Wha'll buy my caller herrin'?
> They're bonnie fish and halesome fairin'
> (Lady Nairne, 1766–1845)

In Scotland, herrings are often tossed in oatmeal before they are fried, and the fish develop tasty, distinctly nutty coats.

Herrin' in Oatmeal

For each serving:
2 herring
Salt and pepper
1oz (28g) oatmeal
1oz (28g) dripping, or butter if preferred

Clean and trim the fish, and dry in a clean cloth. Make a couple of cuts in each side. Season well and toss in the oatmeal until well coated. Heat the dripping in a frying pan and when it begins to smoke toss in the herring. Fry for about 10min on each side, or until well browned. Shake off excess fat and serve garnished with a lemon wedge or parsley.

White pudding, or mealie jamie as it was once known, was made as early as the fifteenth century. The puddings were originally boiled in tripe skins and stored for months on end amongst the oats in the meal chest. However, the old recipe can be successfully boiled in a pudding cloth, or steamed in a basin.

White Pudding or Mealie Jamie

1½lb (675g) oatmeal
1lb (450g) shredded suet
3 medium onions, finely chopped
2–3tsp salt
1tsp Jamaica pepper

Lay the oatmeal on a baking sheet and toast under the grill or in a hot oven. Mix with all the other ingredients and tie securely, allowing room for expansion, in a pudding cloth, or put in a greased pudding basin. Boil for 1hr. This pudding is reputed to keep for ages providing it is kept bone dry.

When required, reheat, or fry hunks of the pudding. It is good with stews – put dumplings of it in the stewpot for the last 20 min cooking time – and goes well with most meats. The same ingredients also make an interesting stuffing for chickens and turkeys.

Similar in that it is traditionally encased in an animal stomach skin, but far more celebrated than the white pudding, is the Haggis. Few visitors leave Scotland without having sampled a bit of real Scottish Haggis.

Haggis was in fact very popular in England (see Northumberland section) from a very early age up to the beginning of the eighteenth century, where it was also known as 'hagas' or 'habbys'. The exact origin of the word haggis has many possibilities. It may have been formed, like the word hash, from the French *hachis*, meaning to chop. Alternatively, it could be a corruption of either the Anglo-Saxon word *haecan* – to chop into pieces – or from to *hag* – an old word meaning to hack.

Even Queen Victoria munched through a haggis when she stayed with the Duchess of Atholl at Blair Castle, and wrote that she liked it very much.

Although described by W. E. Henky as 'a gallimaufray of offal', and metaphorically as 'a bellyful of Burns', a haggis is really a glorified sausage. Incidentally, years ago, the name pudding was far more accommodating and described sausages as well as steamed afters and the like. This explains the odd sixteenth-century saying: 'everything has an end but a pudding has two' and also the mother's request that her child 'must eat another yard of pudding', in other words be older, before gaining a certain privilege.

The Haggis Joke Brigade still fool unknowing souls with stories of the Haggis being a wild animal living on the moors, and by issuing invitations for 'Haggis Hunts'. You have been warned!

Haggis makers Lawson of Dyce have been making haggis for years to an old secret recipe, the main ingredients being heart, lung and liver (pluck) minced and mixed with fat, oatmeal, onion and seasoning, and boiled in ox lungs or sheep's maw (stomach). Lawson's directions for cooking haggis specify that it should never be boiled, but placed in cold water and simmered gently. To insure against a disastrous burst in the pan, the haggis can be wrapped in foil before cooking. It should be served piping hot and in Scotland large quantities are served on St Andrew's Day and at Burns' Night celebrations.

The following recipe for those who feel able to stomach the procedure at home is by Meg Dods (author of *The Cook and Housewife's Manual*, Edinburgh, 1826), who once won the first prize in a haggis competition in Edinburgh.

Haggis

Clean a sheep's heart thoroughly. Make incisions in the heart and liver to allow the blood to flow out, and parboil the whole, letting the windpipe lie over the side of the pot to permit the discharge of any remaining impurities; the water may be changed after a few minutes' boiling for fresh water. A half hour's boiling will be sufficient; put back half of the liver to boil until it is soft and will grate easily; take the heart, half of the liver and part of the lites, trim away all skins and mince together. Mince also a pound of good beef suet and four or more onions. Grate the other half of the liver. Add half a dozen small onions peeled and scalded in two waters to mix with this mince. Have prepared some finely ground oatmeal, toasted slowly before the fire for hours till it is a light brown colour and perfectly dry. Less than two teacupsful of meal will do for this quantity of meat. Spread the mince on a board and strew the meal lightly over it, with a high seasoning of pepper, salt and a little cayenne, first well mixed.

Have a Haggis bag (i.e. a sheep's paunch) perfectly clean and see there is no thin part in it, else your whole labour will be lost by its bursting. Some cooks use two bags, one as an outer case. Put in the meat with a good half-pint of beef gravy, or as much strong broth as will make it a very thick stew. Be careful not to fill the bag too full, but allow the meat room to swell; add the juice of a lemon or a little vinegar; press out the air and sew up the bag, prick it with a large needle when it first swells in the pot to prevent bursting. Let it simmer for three hours if large.

Commercially, haggis is available in tins, and a plastic bag is sometimes used in lieu of the sheep's stomach. Lawsons sent me the following jingle (with apologies to Robbie Burns):

> Fair fa your honest sonsie face,
> Great chieftain o' the puddin' race
> We'll see ye next in outer space,
> In plastic skin.
> How unworthy! A damned disgrace,
> It's a muckle sin!

In the past haggis was often made from a pig's stomach by the farm labourer who was lucky enough to receive the stomach after a pig killing. The stomach was turned inside-out, soaked in salted water, and then stuffed with potatoes, onion, sage, oatmeal, and whatever the poor hungry chap could lay his hands on.

Oatmeal's usefulness is not limited to porridge and savoury fare. It is used in a beverage (see Atholl section) and in the dessert known as cranachan or cream-crowdie.

Cranachan or Cream–Crowdie

Whip ½ pint (280ml) cream until frothy. Stir 2–3tbsp of toasted oatmeal into the cream, and sugar to taste. Vanilla or rum flavouring can also be added if desired.

Scottish soups are quite substantial dishes, more akin to stews than thin soups, and Scotch Broth is no exception. This broth is now generally made with neck of mutton, but in times of hardship a marrowbone suffices admirably. In 1786, Boswell wrote in his *Journal of a Tour to the Hebrides with Samuel Johnson* after noting that Johnson had enjoyed several plates of the broth: 'I said, "You never ate it before?". Johnson – "No sir; but I don't care how soon I eat it again".'

Scotch Broth or Barley Broth   (Serves 6)

2lb (900g) neck of mutton
4 pints (2.240l) water
3oz (84g) barley
1tsp salt
1 turnip, diced
1 carrot, diced
1 onion, sliced
4tbsp peas
½ centre heart of small, white cabbage, shredded

Trim the meat and put in a pan with the water, barley and a good teaspoon of salt. Bring to the boil, and boil gently for

1hr. Skim the surface and add the prepared turnip, carrot, onion and peas. Simmer for another hour and add the shredded cabbage. Boil for another 10min, and serve very hot.

Another Scottish soup, Cock-a-leekie, is described in the Edinburgh section.

Scotch Eggs are popular fare all over Britain, especially in pubs, and are believed to have been introduced from France in the early nineteenth century. Much French and Scottish fare is linked, partially because both are old Celtic countries.

Scotch Eggs

For each 4 eggs:
1 beaten egg
12oz (337g) pork sausagemeat
1 level tsp mace
Seasoned breadcrumbs

Hard boil the eggs. Immerse in cold water to stop black rings from forming round the yolks, and shell. Work the mace into the sausagemeat. Dip each egg into the beaten egg and encase in sausagemeat. Dip in the beaten egg again and roll in the seasoned breadcrumbs. Heat a deep pan of oil and drop in the sausagemeat wrapped eggs, a couple at a time. Fry until golden brown and drain well. A chip basket can be used. The Scotch Eggs are eaten either hot or cold, and are especially suitable for picnics as they can be eaten without knives and forks.

More French influence – stoved comes from the French *étuve* and Howtowdie is a corruption of *hutaudeau*, old French for a pullet – and more eggs – Drappit Eggs are just dropped in water to poach. This recipe is very Scottish and an unusual way of serving chicken.

Stoved Howtowdie Wi' Drappit Eggs   (Serves 6)

1 3½–4lb (1.800kg) chicken
Breadcrumb stuffing, with herbs if liked
4oz (112g) butter
8 spring onions
2 cloves
1tsp chicken spice
1 pint (560ml) giblet stock
2lb (900g) spinach
6 medium eggs
1 chicken liver

First get a giblet stock on the go with all the chicken bits and pieces except the liver. Prepare some breadcrumb stuffing and spoon into the carcass. Put the butter in a casserole and leave in the oven to melt. Chop the spring onions, white parts only, and colour in the butter. Put in the stuffed chicken and colour the bottom and both sides for 5min each. Add the cloves and chicken spice and season well with salt and pepper. Spoon the melted butter, onions and seasonings over the bird several times. Add the strained hot giblet stock and put lid on casserole. Cook at 350°F (180°C; Gas mark 4) for an hour or until the flesh is tender. Meanwhile clean the spinach and boil for 5min with a pinch of salt. There should be sufficient moisture on the washed leaves so do not add any more water. Drain and stir in a knob of butter and keep warm. Remove the chicken from the casserole and place on a large serving dish. Arrange the spinach round the edge and keep warm. Strain the chicken stock into a saucepan. Bring to the boil and drop in the eggs, 3 at a time, to poach until set. Scoop these out with a perforated spoon and place on the spinach. Chop the liver very finely and add to the boiling stock. Boil rapidly to reduce and thicken a bit, and then pour over the chicken.

No Scottish Hogmanay is complete without shortbread, and the traditional recipe, along with an unusual wedding custom, can be found in the Shetland section. Petticoat Tails are a kind of shortbread, albeit slightly thinner and crisper than the traditional shortbread, and their fascinating name is believed by some to have originated from their resemblance in shape to the bell-hoop petticoats worn by court ladies. However, other authorities prefer to explain their name as a corruption of *petites gatelles* – French for little cakes.

Petticoat Tails

10oz (280g) flour
2oz (56g) rice flour
5oz (140g) butter
4tbsp milk
2oz (56g) sugar
Caster sugar for sprinkling

Sieve the flours together and make a well in the middle. Melt the butter in the milk, and pour into the well. Add the sugar and mix to a dough with the fingers. Do not work more than necessary. Turn onto a floured board and knead a little – not too much or your shortbread will not be short. Gently roll into a circle about ¼in thick. Cover with a dinner plate and neatly trim to a perfect round. Place an inverted glass in the centre and cut a small round. Keeping the latter unmarked, cut the outer ring into 8 segments, or petticoat tails. Bake all the pieces on greased trays at 350°F (180°C; Gas mark 4) for 20–25min, or until they are golden. Petticoat tails are generally browned more than ordinary shortbread. Leave to cool before re-assembling the pattern on a large plate or round tray. Sprinkle with caster sugar if very sweet biscuits are liked.

A bun is an old Scottish word used to describe a plum cake, and Black Bun is a very rich fruit cake made especially for the convivial celebrations at Hogmanay. Robert Louis Stevenson described the cake as 'a black substance inimical to life'. The cake is encased in a pastry shell during baking to keep the juices and flavour from escaping, and this was originally intended to be discarded when the bun was eaten.

Scottish Black Bun

PASTRY CASE
8oz (225g) butter or margarine
1lb (450g) flour
Water
Beaten egg for glaze
BUN MIX
1lb (450g) plain flour
2tsp cinnamon
1tsp ground ginger
1tsp nutmeg
1tsp salt
1tsp baking soda
6oz (170g) brown sugar
2lb (900g) currants
2lb (900g) muscatel raisins
8oz (225g) blanched and chopped almonds
8oz (225g) mixed candied peel
2tbsp brandy
Little milk

Rub the butter into the flour to make a breadcrumb mix. Add sufficient water to make a workable paste. Roll out on a floured board and line a large round cake tin, which has been greased and floured, saving enough pastry for a lid. To make the filling, sieve the flour with the spices, soda and salt. Mix with the sugar, currants, raisins, almonds and peel. Add the brandy and just enough milk to make a very stiff cake mixture. Spoon into the pastry lined tin and flatten the top with the back of the spoon. Dampen top edges of pastry shell and position lid. Pinch edges to seal. Prick all over the top with a fork and make one or two incisions, right down to the base, with a meat skewer. Brush with beaten egg. Bake at 350°F (180°C; Gas mark 4) for about 3hr.

At Hogmanay gatherings, great slices of Black Bun are traditionally washed down with many het pints. Years ago, it was customary to carry gallons of the New Year brew through the streets in great copper toddy-kettles. Sir Walter Scott is quoted as saying that the welcoming of a New Year without 'the immemorial liberation of a het pint' would have been 'very uncomfortable'.

Het Pint

4 pints (2.240l) mild ale
2 level tsp ground nutmeg
3oz (84g) sugar
3 eggs, beaten
½ pint (280ml) Scotch whisky

Pour ale into a pan, add nutmeg and bring almost, but not quite, to the boil. Remove from heat and stir in sugar to dissolve. Let it cool a bit before very gradually stirring in the beaten eggs. Add the whisky and return to a low heat to heat up, but on no account allow it to boil. Take another pan and pour the brew from one pan to the other until it becomes smooth and glossy. Drink.

Whisky

'Freedom and Whisky gang together' wrote Burns, and by the end of the poet's life in 1796, there were 1,000 illicit stills producing the 'water of life' in Scotland. It was not until 1824 that one distiller, George Smith of Glenlivet, took the first steps to legalise whisky by becoming licensed. There are now numerous whisky distillers in Scotland, from those producing the single malt, unblended varieties in the Highlands, to the better known large concerns producing the carefully blended whiskies. The choice is yours. Visitors to Scotland have the pleasure of being able to follow 'Whisky Trails' and many of the distillers open their premises for nosing and 'niffing.

Scotch Beef is mentioned under Aberdeen; for Cheese see Dunlop, and Tain, where the cheese-making business, reviving many old Scottish recipes, was only commenced a decade or so ago.

IRELAND

The Emerald Isle – so called because of the blanket of lush, green countryside that the towns have barely disturbed – has a wealth of fare to offer her visitors and inhabitants alike. The name Irish has become attached to numerous foods which command worldwide fame. Most people have at sometime been acquainted with Irish Stew and Soda Bread, and the regional Limerick Ham, Kerry Butter and Dublin Bay Prawns. The rivers are well stocked with fish (Shannon Salmon is an especial delight), the numerous dairy farms ensure a good dairy market, and cattle are plentiful. However, it is with the humble potato or murphy that Irish cooking is most commonly associated. The Irish have been born and bred on murphies ever since Sir Walter Raleigh first cultivated them on his County Cork estate in 1585 and they have sustained many an Irish peasant through the oppressive years in Ireland's troubled history. It was only the unexpected failure of the potato crop that resulted in the dreadful Black Famine in the last century.

The Irish invariably cook potatoes in their skins. Wise of course since most of the vegetable's goodness is found directly below the skin and an over enthusiastic peeler throws all this away. Years ago, murphies were boiled in their skins in farmhouse bastable ovens. Then they were drained and the oven cooking pot transferred from its suspension over the fire, to a pot-hole in the floor. This was to enable the potatoes to be beetled or mashed without the pot wobbling all over the place, and it is believed to be the origin of the word pot-hole. Later bastables, however, sometimes had four feet which made the pot-holes obsolete. It is still customary, in many parts of the world, to nickname Irishmen with the surname Murphy, Spud!

Boxty is a traditional Irish potato dish which is still made today. Maybe it is this old rhyme that keeps it so popular.

> Boxty on the griddle, boxty in the pan,
> The wee one in the middle, is for Mary Ann.
> Boxty on the griddle, boxty in the pan,
> If you don't eat boxty, you'll never get a man.

Originally boxty was served on the eve of All Saints' Day – Hallowe'en – but any desperate spinsters may as well get cooking straight away.

Griddle Boxty or Boxty Bread   (Makes 2)

1lb (450g) raw potatoes
1lb (450g) boiled mashed potatoes
1lb (450g) plain flour
1tsp baking soda
Salt and pepper
5oz (140g) melted butter
Milk for glaze

Peel the raw potatoes and grate them onto a clean cloth. Hold the edges of the cloth and gently squeeze the potato juice into a bowl. Leave the bowl on one side until the starch sinks, about ½hr. Mix the gratings with the boiled, mashed potato, flour, soda, shake of salt and pepper and melted butter. Carefully pour off the potato water and stir the starch into the mixture. Knead on a floured board and shape into 2 large rounds. Mark into farls or quarters, brush with a little milk and place on a baking tray. Bake in an oven pre-heated to 350°F (180°C; Gas mark 4) for 50min. Alternatively, they can be cooked on a griddle (without glaze) for about 15–20min each side.

Pan Boxty or Boxty Pancakes

These are made from the same ingredients as Boxty Bread plus enough milk to make a batter consistency. Drop tablespoons of the batter into a hot oiled frying pan and fry on both sides until lightly browned. Serve them straight from the pan with a jug of melted butter and a bowl of brown sugar.

Another Irish potato speciality is Potato and Apple Cake. This is traditionally served hot at tea time in the northern counties and shows how versatile the Irish have made their potatoes, this time turning them into pastry.

Irish Potato and Apple Cake

POTATO PASTRY
1lb (450g) boiled potatoes
1oz (28g) margarine
½oz (14g) caster sugar
Pinch of salt
4oz (112g) plain flour
Milk
APPLE FILLING
1lb (450g) cooking apples, peeled and sliced
1oz (28g) melted butter
Sugar to taste

Drain the boiled potatoes and push them through a sieve. Mash with margarine, sugar and salt. Stir in the flour to make a dough. Turn out onto a floured board and knead until smooth. Divide pastry in half and roll out into 2 rounds to fit a pie plate. Grease plate and cover with one round. Trim and brush edge with milk. Lay the prepared apple slices in the centre and pour the melted butter over. Sprinkle to taste with sugar. Position the pastry cover. Trim and pinch edges together. Make 3 slits in the top to let steam escape and brush lightly with milk. Bake in an oven pre-heated to 375°F (190°C; Gas mark 5) for about 40min.

Champ and Colcannon also are famous potato recipes. Champ is a favourite with children and they even have a rhyme about it.

> There was an old woman who lived in a lamp,
> She had no room to beetle her champ.
> She up'd with her beetle and broke the lamp,
> And now she has room to beetle her champ!

'To beetle her champ' refers to the beetle, a wooden pestle type implement, which was used to pound the potatoes in days gone by.

Irish Champ   (Serves 3-4)
1lb (450g) freshly boiled potatoes
6 scallions or spring onions
¼ pint (140ml) milk
Salt and pepper
4oz (112g) butter

Drain the boiled potatoes well and cover the saucepan with a cloth to absorb the steam. Chop the scallions finely, using both the green and white parts, and boil them in milk for a few minutes. Mash the dried, boiled potatoes (if they are at all wet, the dish will be spoilt) and season well with salt and pepper. Pour in the milk and scallions and beat vigorously. Serve large mounds of the champ in individual bowls. Make a dip in each mound and add a generous knob of butter. The dish is eaten on its own and children like to dip the dry potato mixture into the pool of melted butter.

Colcannon

Colcannon is a typical Irish Hallowe'en dish to which miniature charms are often added as a novelty. If the eater finds a gold ring he or she will marry in the year, and a horseshoe and sixpence forecast luck and wealth respectively. Alas, the finders of buttons or thimbles are fated never to marry. The recipe is the same as for Champ but with the addition of 1lb (450g) of boiled kale or cabbage. This is chopped and blended with the potato.

If you find breadmaking with yeast time consuming, you will appreciate the speed with which Soda Bread is made. As it does not keep very well, it is still made each day on many Irish farms, and eaten, no doubt, straight from the oven smothered with fresh farm butter.

Irish Soda Bread

1lb (450g) wholewheat flour
8oz (225g) plain white flour
1tsp salt
1tsp bicarbonate of soda
½ pint (280ml) buttermilk or soured milk

Combine the flours with the salt and soda and pour in the buttermilk or soured milk in stages. Mix to make a soft dough. With floured hands, knead the dough lightly on a floured board, and shape into a flat round about 9in in diameter. Mark the top with a cross, using a floured knife, and stand on a baking sheet. Bake in an oven preheated to 425°F (220°C; Gas mark 7) for about ½hr. It is sufficiently baked if it sounds hollow when tapped underneath.

White soda bread is made as above by substituting white flour for the wholewheat flour, using 1½lb (675g) in all.

As Irish cooks have perfected breadmaking without yeast, it seems odd that their fruit bread, known as Barm Brack, traditionally calls for the use of yeast. This tea bread –

similar to Anglesey's Bara Brith – is another Irish Hallowe'en speciality, and like Colcannon, a golden ring is sometimes added to determine who shall wed before the year is out.

Barm Brack

½oz (14g) dried yeast
1tsp sugar
½ pint warm milk and water mixed
1lb (450g) plain flour
1tsp salt
2oz (56g) butter
3oz (84g) sugar
1 egg
2oz (56g) currants
2oz (56g) raisins
2oz (56g) sultanas
2oz (56g) mixed candied peel
Melted butter

Mix the yeast with half of the warm (blood heat) milk and water and the 1tsp of sugar. Leave to froth. Sieve the flour and salt, and rub in the butter. Mix in the sugar and make a well. Beat the egg with the remaining milk and water and pour, with the activated yeast liquid, into the well. Stir in the dried fruits and mix to a dough. Cover with an oiled polythene sheet and leave in a warmish place to double in size. Turn onto a board and knead for several minutes. Shape into a loaf and place in a lightly greased and floured loaf tin. Leave to prove again for about 20min. Then bake at 425°F (220°C; Gas mark 7) for about 50min–1hr. Brush the top with melted butter while the bread is still warm. Serve sliced, with butter if liked, at tea time. When it gets a bit stale it is still good toasted.

The most universally known of all Irish dishes is surely Irish Stew. This is a plain and simple casserole which is quite delicious. Nowadays neck of lamb is generally used, ranging from scrag to best end, and it is only personal preference, or purse, that decides. However, years ago, farmers considered their lambs far too valuable to be used in stews and presented their wives with kid meat instead. The stew was cooked in a bastable oven over a peat fire and hot embers were placed on the lid from time to time, to ensure the even distribution of the heat. Unlike many of the cauldron-type stewpots of yesteryear, the Irish bastables were also used for baking, hence the lid.

The art of cooking the stew is to prevent as much evaporation as possible. Originally this was done by covering the top of the stew with a flour and water paste before positioning the lid. This pastry topping was discarded – probably thrown to any farm animal who would demolish it with relish – before the stew was served.

Irish Stew   (Serves 4–6)

3lb (1.350kg) neck of lamb (scrag, middle or best end)
2lb (900g) potatoes
1lb (450g) onions
1tsp thyme
Salt
Black pepper
½–¾ pint (280–420ml) water

Remove any excess fat and gristle from the lamb and cut into smallish pieces. Some cooks like to discard the bone but it is better to include it as it adds to the flavour. Peel the potatoes and halve if large. Peel and slice the onions. Layer the lamb, potatoes and onions in a casserole, sprinkling with thyme and seasoning with salt and black pepper at intervals. Finish with a layer of potatoes on top. Pour in the water and cover with foil, pulling it taut over the pot. Put on lid. Cook at 350°F (180°C; Gas mark 4) for 2½hr or until the meat is tender. Alternatively the stew can be cooked on top of the stove for the same length of time. Traditional accompaniments to Irish Stew are boiled carrots and pickled red cabbage. But any vegetables should be cooked separately, not in with the stew.

When it comes to beverages, the Irish prefer to drink tea throughout the day, as opposed to coffee. However when they do take coffee they really go to town – the celebrated Irish Coffee is an unforgettable indulgence.

Irish Coffee

For each serving:
Double measure Irish whiskey
Strong black coffee, sweetened with brown sugar
1½tbsp cream

First warm some stemmed glasses by rinsing them in a bowl of hot water and drying quickly. Pour in whiskey, then fill up the glass to within an inch of the rim with hot, sweetened, black coffee. Finally pour the cream carefully over the back of a spoon so that it floats temptingly on top. Do not stir, but sip the whiskeyed coffee through the cream.

Irish whiskey, with an 'e', is not met in other parts of

Britain as frequently as Scotch whisky, without an 'e'. This does not mean that it is any the less commendable. Irish whiskey is pot-stilled as a rule and made from barley, wheat and rye, as is usual, with the addition of the Irish peculiarity, oats. Not much blending is possible as there are only half a dozen or so large distilleries. By law, Irish whiskey must have matured for seven years before it can be offered for sale.

One of Ireland's whiskey distillers, situated in Tullamore, is also responsible for producing the liqueur, Irish Mist, which is based on heather honey and whiskey. The distillers call it 'Ireland's legendary liqueur' and indeed, it does have a quaint legend behind it. The story begins many centuries ago when ancient Ireland was governed by warring clans. These warriors drank a heather wine, the recipe for which was kept secret. When Ireland was invaded by the Danes and Normans, the Irish inhabitants fled overseas taking the heather wine recipe with them. This hurried emigration has often been called 'the flight of the wild geese' and occurred during the sixteenth century. ' 'Twas a sad loss for Ireland', Daniel E. Williams, a distiller at Tullamore in the last century, is alleged to have lamented, and his successors searched in vain for the recipe for over a century. Then in 1948, an Austrian refugee brought a recipe of Irish origin, that had been in his family for many years, into the Tullamore distillery. This turned out to be the recipe which the Williams family had been searching for and they subsequently distilled it under the name Irish Mist. It is now exported to eighty-five different countries. The liqueur is a useful addition to any cocktail cabinet and the following recipe is taken from the company's leaflet.

Irish Mist on the Rocks ('Misty')

Pour 2 jiggers Irish Mist liqueur over clear cubed ice in an on-the-rocks glass; garnish of lime, orange, or cherry, at your discretion.

> Health and long life to you,
> Land without rent to you,
> A child every year to you,
> And may you die in Ireland.
> (Trad Irish toast)

When it comes to beer, it is the stout variety that the Irish live on: Guinness dominates the Irish market. It began when Arthur Guinness (one of many of that name) decided to set himself up in business with a £100 legacy. In 1756 he established a brewery in Leixlip, Co Kildare. Three years later, he moved to St James Gate in Dublin and signed a

lease for 9,000 years at £45pa. In those days the brewery consisted of a mill, copper kieve, a couple of malthouses and modest stables. At first things were difficult as there was not a great deal of enthusiasm for beer and in much of rural Ireland there was no monetary system to speak of. Thus sales were primarily confined to Dublin and only ale and table beer were brewed. However, by the end of the century business was thriving and ales were superseded by porter, a lighter stout than Guinness. The brewery has been passed from father to son right up to the present day. There have been the invariable ups and downs but now the Dublin brewery is the largest in Europe. The taste of Guinness has become so popular that it is now brewed in a dozen different countries and sold in about 140. All these concerns have been instigated by the Irish brewery. In Ireland, Guinness is now the largest private employer, and of the '8 million glasses enjoyed each day' 4 million are brewed at St James Gate.

Guinness stout is made from barley, hops, yeast and water by a natural process that has barely altered over the last two centuries. The only difference between the original porter and Guinness is that the latter is stronger. It is only in the past year or so that the brewing of porter has ceased, as apparently there is no longer a demand for the milder drink. Irish cooks frequently added porter to many recipes – Porter Cake and Plum Pudding are prime examples. Nowadays Guinness is substituted and the following recipes were kindly sent to me by the Guinnesses in Dublin.

Mr Guinness's Cake

8oz (225g) butter
8oz (225g) soft brown sugar
4 eggs, lightly beaten
10oz (280g) plain flour sieved with 2 level tsp mixed spice
8oz (225g) seedless raisins
8oz (225g) sultanas
4oz (112g) mixed peel
4oz (112g) walnuts (chopped)
8–12tbsp Guinness

Cream butter and sugar together until light and creamy. Gradually beat in the eggs. Fold in the flour and mixed spice. Add the raisins, sultanas, mixed peel and walnuts. Mix well together. Stir 4tbsp Guinness into the mixture and mix to a soft dropping consistency. Turn into a prepared 7in round cake tin and bake at 325°F (170°C; Gas mark 3) for 1hr. Then reduce heat to 300°F (150°C; Gas mark 2) and cook for another 1½hr. Allow to become cold. Remove from cake tin. Prick the base of the cake with a skewer, and spoon over the remaining 4–8tbsp Guinness. Keep cake for one week before eating.

Mr Guinness's Christmas Pudding

10oz (280g) fresh breadcrumbs
8oz (225g) soft brown sugar
8oz (225g) currants
10oz (280g) seeded raisins, chopped
8oz (225g) sultanas
2oz (56g) mixed peel, chopped
10oz (280g) shredded suet
½ level tsp salt
1 level tsp mixed spice
Grated rind of 1 lemon
1dsp lemon juice
2 large eggs, beaten
¼ pint (140ml) milk
½ pint (280ml) Guinness

Mix together in a large basin all dry ingredients. Stir in lemon juice, eggs, milk and Guinness. Mix well and turn into two 2½ pint well greased pudding basins. Tie pudding cloths over puddings, or cover them tightly with greaseproof paper and foil. Leave overnight. Steam for about 7½hr. If not eating the pudding immediately, cool, re-cover and store in a cool place. When required, steam for a further 2–3hr before serving. (This quantity serves 10–12 people.)

ABERDEEN

Fish Market

Aberdeen, a coastal university city in Scotland's Grampian region, has a thriving fishing industry. It really is well worth getting up very early to go and watch the bidding which starts around 7.30 am – even though much of the fishermen's jargon sounds like an unlearnable foreign language. Before the Victoria Bridge was built over the river in 1881 the two fishing communities – the Footdee (which sounds more like 'Fitty') on the north bank, and the Torry on the south – remained quite separate from each other and were more grimly competitive than they are nowadays.

The fishing market is a scene of non-stop bustle and colourful agitation – the weather-worn crews, returning from up to a week at sea, don shapeless, brightly coloured oilskins and large squelchy wellies, and sort out endless boxes of bored-looking fish into some sort of order for the prospective buyers. Herring, haddock, halibut, sole, cod, plaice, rock salmon, whiting – even the ugly monk-fish with its mouth ready for the dentist – await their turn for auction, their skins silvery wet and sequinned with sunlight. The trawlers nudging each other in their mooring spaces look battered and weary. However, the atmosphere is a happy, hard working one, unmistakably tainted with the smell of freshly caught fish.

Fish is featured in many Scottish recipes: see the Arbroath section for smokies, and the Scotland section for the classic herrin' in oatmeal.

Aberdeen has a special recipe for the little butter rolls known as buttery rowies. These were once sold on the streets and an old Aberdeen street cry 'bawbee baps and buttery rowies' is still remembered.

Buttery Rowies   (Makes 20–25)

1lb (450g) strong plain flour
1tsp salt
1oz (28g) baker's yeast
1 level tbsp caster sugar
¾ pint (420ml) approx tepid water

34

5oz (140g) butter
5oz (140g) lard

Sift the flour and salt into a bowl. Cream the yeast and sugar together and add to the sifted flour with sufficient warm water to mix to a soft elastic dough. Cover and leave in a warmish place to double in size. Mash the butter and lard together until well blended, and divide into 3 parts. Roll the risen dough out to make a long oblong. Dot with one-third of the fat, fold into 3 (as in flaky pastry making) and roll out again. Repeat twice more with remaining fat. Cut into ovals and place on a lightly greased and floured baking tray. Leave to prove again for 30min. Bake in an oven preheated to 400°F (200°C; Gas mark 6) for 20–25min.

Beef

Aberdeen beef is noted all over the world and comes from the pedigree breed of black, hornless cattle known as the Aberdeen Angus. Ideally, the animals should be slaughtered before they are eighteen months old, to produce the superb, sought-after steaks. One old Scottish recipe calls for 3lb of rump steak and 2 dozen oysters. The steak, which should be in one piece, is slit horizontally to make an envelope in which the oysters are stuffed. It is then sewn up, dusted with flour and seasoning, deep fried until browned, and finally stewed in a stock until cooked through.

More popular for the average family – not in the caviare class – is the old Aberdeen Sausage recipe.

Aberdeen Sausage   (Serves 4–6)

1 large onion
4oz (112g) streaky bacon
1lb (450g) minced beef
4oz (112g) rolled oats
1 small egg, beaten
1tbsp Worcestershire sauce
1tbsp chopped parsley
Salt and pepper

Peel the onio nand de-rind the bacon. Mince both and add to the minced beef. Stir in the rolled oats, egg, Worcestershire sauce, and parsley, and season well with salt and pepper. Shape the mixture into a big sausage and wrap in a piece of oiled foil. Twist ends to secure and bake in an oven preheated to 325°F (170°C; Gas mark 3) for about 2hr. The sausage can be sliced and served hot, but is equally tasty eaten cold as a picnic meat, in which case it should be kept in the refrigerator in its foil wrapping until required.

ANGLESEY

Egg Clapping

On the Monday before Easter on the island of Anglesey, children are in their element as they are actually encouraged to be noisy for the sake of maintaining a local custom. Traditionally, they go around clapping wooden clappers – similar to castanets – and at the same time chanting, 'Clap, clap, an egg for little boys on the parish', only in Welsh of course. The custom stems from the old belief that eggs at Easter symbolise fertility.

The recipe for Anglesey eggs is very suitable for the Welsh kitchen as it includes leeks – one of the Welsh national emblems.

Anglesey Eggs   (Serves 3–4)

6 leeks
12oz (337g) mashed potato
1½oz (42g) butter
Salt and pepper
6 eggs, hard boiled
SAUCE
½oz (14g) butter
½oz (14g) flour
½ pint (280ml) milk
3oz (84g) grated cheese
Salt and pepper

Leave the leeks to soak in cold water, in advance, and much of the dirt will be drawn out. Scrub them, and chop into pieces. Cook in boiling, salted water until tender, about 10min. Drain thoroughly and mash with the potato, butter and seasoning until well mixed and fluffy. Spoon the mixture round the edge of an oval oven dish. Cut the hard boiled eggs into halves, or smaller pieces if preferred, and put in the middle of the leek and potato mash. Keep warm under grill or in the oven.
Make the sauce. Melt the butter in a saucepan, add the flour and beat to make a roux. Gradually add the milk, and then stir in 2oz (56g) of the grated cheese. Season to taste and pour the sauce over the chopped eggs and mash. Sprinkle the remaining cheese over the dish and return to a hot grill or oven. Heat until the cheese is sizzling and golden brown.

Speckled Bread or Bara Brith

Many kinds of speckled bread are made all over Wales – some

with yeast, some without, some with egg, some without. This Anglesey recipe, donated by a farmer's wife, is without yeast – ' 'Tis better this way' – but with an egg.

6oz (168g) currants
6oz (168g) sultanas
8oz (225g) soft brown sugar
1 cup hot, milkless tea
3oz (84g) butter
1lb (450g) self-raising flour
Pinch of salt
1 egg, beaten

Mix the dried fruit with the sugar and pour the hot tea over. Leave overnight, if possible, for the fruit to plump itself out. Rub the butter into the flour and salt, and add the egg. Mix in the soaked fruit. Grease and line a 2lb loaf tin, put the mixture in the tin and bake in an oven preheated to 350°F (180°C; Gas mark 4) for 1½hr, or until well done.

An old Welsh custom revolves around this speckled bread, ensuring good luck and fortune for those who observe it. A dark-haired man has to leave the house by the back door, a few minutes before midnight on New Year's Eve. He has to return through the front door, in the first minutes of the New Year, with a lump of coal in his pocket. This ritual is known as first-footing and is practised in other places besides Wales. However in Wales, the first-footer exchanges his dirty lump of coal for a generous slice of bara brith!

ABROATH

Smokies

Odd though it may be, the Scottish haddocks known as Arbroath smokies did not originate in Arbroath, but in the nearby fishing village of Auchmithie. It was there that the local folk learnt to poke little wooden sticks into the haddocks' gills and to hang them, tied tail to tail, in pairs over wooden spits high in the old lums or chimneys. Then, as smokies became popular, special smoke pits were sunk in the ground and the haddocks were hung over halved whisky barrels and smoked over chips of wood – usually oak or silver birch. The history of Arbroath smokies is described by F. Marian McNeill in her book *The Scots Kitchen*. The author goes on to explain how a community of Auchmithie fisher folk moved to Arbroath at the beginning of the nineteenth century and continued their practice of smoking haddock. However the industry did not develop much until the end of the nineteenth century, by which time Auchmithie smokies had adopted the new name Arbroath smokies.

These small cured haddocks are sometimes called close haddocks as they are smoked whole instead of being split and flattened like Finnan Haddocks or Haddies (see Findon). Some people eat the fish cold, with bread and butter, for breakfast or high tea, but the following recipe is worth sampling.

Grilled Smokies

Arbroath Smokies (2 per person)
Black pepper
Butter

Warm the fish under a grill, allowing two per person, or three if very hungry, until heated through. Remove and open each fish out. Discard the backbone. Season well with black pepper, and spread generously with butter. Close up and reheat until piping hot. Serve immediately, and get the air freshener out if you are expecting guests, otherwise wallow in a beautiful fishy aroma.

ATHOLL

Just south of the Forest of Atholl, in Scotland, at Blair Atholl lies Blair Castle, the seat of His Grace the Duke of Atholl and the home of Atholl Brose. The whisky-based brose was duly sampled by Queen Victoria and Prince Albert when they visited Blair Atholl in 1844. Sheridan also partook of the beverage, 'rather freely' so it is chronicled, whilst being entertained at Blair Castle.

The Atholl Brose recipe dates from 1475 when the Duke of Atholl, and others, were sent on an expedition to crush the rebellion instigated by John McDonald, Earl of Ross and Lord of the Isles. According to legend, Atholl learned that Ross often drank water from a small well in a local rock, and cunningly devised some means of replacing the water with a honey and whisky mixture. The rebellious Ross fell for the trick, partook freely of the mixture, and subsequently nodded off to the pleasant world of slumber, quite unguarded. When the earl eventually awoke, he found himself captured, and with no option but to surrender himself to the clemency of James III. The Atholl crest and motto, 'Furth, Fortune and Fill the Fetters', also dates from the time of the Ross rebellion. Tradition has it that the King used the words of the motto when assigning the mission to Atholl.

> Aye since he wore the tartan trews
> He dearly lo'ed the Atholl Brose.
>
> (Niel Gow, 1727–1807)

The following recipe was obtained from Blair Castle in 1976.

Atholl Brose

Strain a handful of oatmeal through a fine sieve into a basin and mix with cold water to the consistency of a thick paste. Be careful not to make it too watery. Add 4 dessert spoonfuls of runny honey to 4 sherry glassfuls of the sieved oatmeal. Stir well together and put into a quart bottle. Fill up with whisky. Shake well before serving.

This can be drunk at once or kept indefinitely if well corked and sealed. The bottle should be kept standing upright. Some ladies like a little cream added to it.

AYLESBURY

Aylesbury Ducks

Aylesbury ducks were first bred in the Buckinghamshire town many years ago, but alas, there are no flocks quacking in the place nowadays. They are, however, bred elsewhere. They are the most popular table duck, being unequalled in flavour, but are poor layers. It is the rapid growth of the young ducklings, who often weigh 5lb when only eight or nine weeks old, that produces the succulent flesh and splendid taste. Traditionally, an Aylesbury duck is served with orange sauce.

Aylesbury Duck with Orange Sauce   (Serves 3–4)

1 duck, about 5lb (2.250kg)
1 orange, sliced
Salt
SAUCE
2 oranges
½ pint (280ml) giblet stock
4tbsp duck juices
1tbsp brown sugar
2tbsp redcurrant jelly
2tbsp sherry or brandy
Salt and pepper

Prepare the duck for the oven unless the butcher has already done this. Prick all over the duck with a fork, rub with butter and sprinkle with salt. Roast in an oven preheated to 375°F (190°C; Gas mark 5) allowing 20min per lb plus an extra 15min. Baste from time to time. Boil the neck and giblets to make about ½ pint of stock. Strain. When the duck is ready, arrange on an oven-to-table dish with the orange slices, and keep warm in the oven. Strain the cooking juices and keep on one side. Make the sauce. Grate the rinds from the 2 oranges into a saucepan with as much juice as possible squeezed from the fruit. Add the giblet stock, about 4tbsp of the duck juices, the brown sugar, the redcurrant jelly and the hard stuff. Season. Heat gently, stirring to dissolve the sugar and jelly. Cook until it thickens a bit, and then pour over the roasted duck. Serve immediately.

BAKEWELL

Obvious though it may appear, the name Bakewell does not refer to the famous pudding which originated in the Derbyshire town. Bakewell is in fact derived from an Anglo-Saxon personal name 'Bake', attached to 'well', which refers to the warm water springs in the district.

The Bakewell Pudding was invented by accident, following a misunderstanding between Mrs Greaves, proprietor of the Rutland Arms Hotel in the last century, and her cook. The cook was supposedly preparing a strawberry jam tart, but instead of stirring the egg mixture into the pastry, she poured it on top of the jam. The guests in the hotel complimented the new 'pudding' so profusely, that the inept cook was instructed to make it regularly. The present chef at the Rutland Arms claims to have the original recipe, but of course will not disclose the ingredients. The hotel is also noted for its association with Jane Austen. She is reputed to have taken a room there when she was writing *Pride and Prejudice*, and some say that she actually wrote about Bakewell, calling it Lambton.

Back to the pudding, which incidentally should *never* be

called Bakewell Tart, as some bakers and manufacturers persist in doing. Bakewellians are very sensitive about this! Traditionally, the pudding is oval, although round ones of various sizes are acceptable. Visitors to the town can choose between the two establishments which maintain original pudding traditions: Bloomers in Matlock Street and the Olde Original Bakewell Pudding Shop in the Square.

Bakewell Pudding   (Serves 4–6)

8oz (225g) puff pastry
2–3tbsp strawberry or raspberry jam
3 large eggs
4oz (112g) sugar
4oz (112g) melted butter
1½oz (42g) ground almonds

Grease an oval pudding dish if you have one. If not, use a 6in or 7in round cake tin. Roll out the pastry and line the dish with it. Spread the jam evenly over the base. Beat the eggs with the sugar until frothy, and then gradually pour in the melted butter. Beat well and finally stir in the ground almonds. Pour over jam in pastry and bake in an oven preheated to 400°F (200°C; Gas mark 6), until set and delicately browned – about 35min.

BANBURY

Ride a cock horse to Banbury Cross,
To see a fine lady upon a white horse,
With rings on her fingers and bells on her toes,
She shall have music wherever she goes.

This old rhyme is a favourite with children and a trip to Banbury in Oxfordshire will reward the traveller with the sight of Banbury Cross. Alas, no 'fine lady upon a white horse' can be located, but instead the famous Banbury cakes should console him.

It is known that Banbury cakes were made as early as the sixteenth century. Their production led to another industry: the making of oval cake baskets from willow chips, in which the cakes were sold. Unfortunately, there is little trace of this skilled craft nowadays, although one basket can be seen in Banbury Museum.

The Original Banbury Cake Shop, lastly owned by E. W. Brown Ltd, has sadly been pulled down to make way for development, but the tradition still flourishes; the same family firm produces Banbury cakes at Charlbury, about fifteen miles out from Banbury. The cakes are sold, in packets of three, by many Banbury shopkeepers. In fact it is almost impossible to leave the town without some, unless of course one is being very strict on a reducing diet!

Banbury Cakes   (Makes about 6)

8oz (225g) puff pastry
1oz (28g) butter
½ level tbsp flour
1tbsp rum or sherry
4oz (112g) currants
1oz (28g) mixed, candied peel
1tsp cinnamon
1tsp nutmeg
Milk and sugar

Grease a large baking sheet. Roll out the pastry thinly and cut out oval shapes about 6in × 4in. Melt the butter over a low heat and stir in the flour and rum or sherry. Beat to make a smooth paste and leave to cool a little. Stir in the dried fruits and spices. Mix well and put a tablespoon of the mixture in the middle of each oval. Fold the surrounding pastry over, to enclose the filling, turn over and flatten slightly with a rolling pin, still keeping an oval shape. Make 3 slits in the top. Brush with milk and sprinkle with sugar. Bake at 400°F (200°C; Gas mark 6) for 20 min.

BATH

There can surely be few places that offer as much as Bath. This famous Georgian city boasts many architectural splendours, famous past residents, culinary delights, and the magnificent hot water baths. These unique baths were mostly constructed by the Romans and much of the original bricks and mortar can be seen today. Nearly half a million gallons of water, at a constant temperature of 120°F (48°C), gush up from the natural springs every day. Some is diverted to a small fountain in the Pump Room where visitors are invited to drink it free of charge. You can also take morning coffee or afternoon tea in the Pump Room, and with it one of those delicious Bath buns. The exact origin of these buns is not known, but they are believed to have first been made in the latter half of the nineteenth century. Alfred Taylor (Bath) Ltd of 8–9, New Bond Street, Bath, make excellent Bath buns to their own original recipe, and their 'Old Red House' bakery shop is well worth a visit.

A true Bath bun is made from a very rich, plain dough and, contrary to common belief, does not contain any fruit. Originally caraway seeds and nib sugar were sprinkled on top. Then, as tastes changed, caraway comfits or currants and nib sugar were used instead. But since World War II, caraway comfits have practically disappeared and nowadays only currants and lump sugar are used.

Bath Buns   (Makes about 6)

½ breakfast cup milk
1tsp sugar
½ level tbsp dried yeast
½tsp salt
8oz (225g) plain flour
4oz (112g) butter
1½oz (42g) sugar
2 eggs
1tbsp currants
2tbsp lump sugar

Warm the milk to 110°F (43°C) or 'hand-hot', remove from heat and dissolve the sugar in it. Sprinkle the dried yeast over and break up any clusters with a fork. Leave in a warmish place for 15min to froth. Sift the flour and salt together and rub in the butter. Add the sugar. Beat the eggs – reserve half an egg for glazing – and stir into the flour with the yeast liquid, to make a soft dough. Leave to double in bulk – about ¾hr in a warmish place. Knead the risen dough for several minutes and then shape into buns. Put on a lightly greased and floured baking tray and brush with the reserved beaten egg. Roughly crumble the sugar lumps. Sprinkle these, with the currants, over the buns. Leave to prove for a further 15min. Bake in an oven preheated to 425°F (220°C; Gas mark 7) for about 15min.

Dr Oliver's Biscuits

Bath has had many distinguished residents including Charles Dickens and Jane Austen. Resident, 200 years ago, in Queen Square was the eminent physician Dr William Oliver (1695–1764) who was one of the pioneers of the Royal Mineral Water Hospital in Bath, and inventor of Oliver biscuits. Made from 'finest flour, pure dairy milk, fresh country butter and malt', the biscuits were nutritious, easily digested and deemed to be the perfect Bathonian health food. In 1738, Frederick, Prince of Wales, spoke of 'the quality of your [Dr Oliver's] excellent biscuits' and Richard Nash, in agreement with His Highness, wagered that 'they make even this Bath water tolerable, while cheese becomes ambrosia upon them'. Dr Oliver willed the secret recipe for his biscuits to his trustworthy coachman, Atkins, along with ten sacks of flour and £100 in cash. Subsequently the servant opened a shop in Green Street and quickly made his fortune from sales of the biscuit. Today the biscuits are manufactured by Huntley and Palmers and still bear a representation of Dr Oliver's head. Huntley and Palmers issued the following information in a press release when they took over manufacture of the biscuits from Fortt's in 1963:

> The Bath Olivers will continue to be sold in the easily recognised tins, and the price will remain the same at 3/11d [20p]. To bring them into line with modern trends, however, they will, for the first time, be sold in a 9½oz packet. The wrapper design for this new packet closely follows the tin, and will sell at 2/4d [12p].

Bath Chaps, Polonies

Bath chaps and Bath polonies are two other culinary specialities which are still available from Bathonian butchers today. Bath chaps are made from a pig's cheek and are very lean and tasty. Bath polonies are made from spiced, minced pork and are recognised by their bright red skins.

Meandering to the right of the front of Bath Abbey, you will come across Lilliput Alley where Sally Lunn's house can be found. This house is believed to be the oldest in Bath and was built in 1480. In 1680 the tenancy was granted to a pastry cook and baker, Sally Lunn. Her reputation for excellent cakes soon earned her the patronage of Beau Nash and other distinguished personages of the era. In 1725, the house was bought by Ralph Allen, who was responsible for much rebuilding in Bath around this time, and was possibly used as his first post office. Later it became tea rooms once more, and in the 1930s, extensive renovation was carried out to restore the building and Sally Lunn's original stone ovens were unearthed in the basement. The house is still used as tea and coffee rooms, and hot, toasted Sally Lunns made to the original recipe are served.

Sally Lunns   (Makes four 4in rounds)

Traditionally these are baked in special Sally Lunn or muffin rings of varying sizes. However, cake tins with diameters of about 4in are suitable. Alternatively, larger tins can be used, and the cakes can be halved or quartered for serving.

4tbsp milk
1tsp sugar
Generous ¾ level tbsp dried yeast
14oz (392g) plain flour
1tsp salt
2 small eggs
¼ pint (140ml) single cream or evaporated milk

Gently warm the milk to blood heat, remove from heat, and dissolve the sugar in it. Sprinkle the dried yeast over and leave for 15min until frothy. Sift the flour and salt together. Beat the eggs with the cream or evaporated milk, and add the activated yeast. Pour the liquid into the flour, and stir to make a soft, pliable dough. Leave in a warmish place for about ¾hr, or until the dough has doubled in size. Grease the tins. Knead the risen dough for a few minutes and break off enough to half fill each ring or tin. Leave to prove again, until they have filled the rings – about 15–20min. Bake at 425°F (220°C; Gas mark 7) for 18–20min. The cakes are split and are traditionally served with scalded cream, but are excellent served hot, with butter and strawberry jam.

BEDFORDSHIRE

Orange Rolling

Among the traditions maintained in Bedfordshire is the custom of orange rolling. Enthusiastic orange rollers still assemble on Dunstable Downs each Easter and the age-old orange-rolling custom – said to symbolise rolling the stone away from Christ's tomb – is still carried out. Visitors to Ickwell can see one of the few maypoles remaining in the country.

Bedfordshire's contribution to the kitchen is called the Bedfordshire Clanger – quite a mouthful to say, and to eat! It is a very old recipe and a good example of how workers were given a two-course meal in a single dish. It was popular with men who did not, and still do not, appreciate the numerous wrappings and ties that packed meals usually entail. It is not a fashionable dish today, being a bit on the heavy side; nevertheless it is worth recording for the time when such food comes into favour again.

Bedfordshire Clanger   (Serves 1 hearty eater)

8oz (225g) self-raising flour
4oz (112g) shredded suet
½tsp salt
Milk
4oz (112g) chopped or minced meat
1 small onion, chopped
3tbsp jam or syrup

First brown the chopped onion and meat together in a pan. Mix the flour, suet and salt with enough milk to make a pliable dough. Roll out to make an oblong about ½in thick, having the longer sides facing you. Spread the meat and onion on the left half of the pastry, leaving a 1in margin down the side. Spread the jam or syrup on the right half, leaving a gap between the two fillings and again leave a 1in margin at the side. Roll up like a swiss roll and pinch each end to stop the fillings from oozing out. Wrap up in a floured pudding cloth and tie around the middle to discourage the flavours from mingling unfavourably. Bend the roll gently, if necessary, to fit it into a saucepan, and boil for about 1½hr. The clangers were wrapped in towels to keep them warm, and taken to the farm hands working in the fields. The savoury end was eaten first and the sweet end as a second course.

Warden Pears

The old Bedford Fair once held at Michaelmas was famous for its baked pears. These were served from large earthenware pans into saucers, and were known as 'wardens'. An old street cry was once frequently aired:

> Smoking hot, piping hot,
> Who knows what I've got
> In my pot? Hot baked wardens.
> All hot! All hot! All hot!

It has been suggested that warden pears may have been named after the Bedfordshire town of Wardon, or after Walden Abbey where pears were successfully cultivated by the Cistercian monks. These baked pears were commonly hawked in the county's streets, particularly in the winter, until the 1860s.

BLACKBURN

Blackburn in Lancashire was once well known for its Fig – or Fag as they were sometimes called – pies. Some of the older inhabitants can still recall the time when Mothering Sunday was known as Fig Sunday, and many locally grown figs were consumed both fresh and in pies and puddings.

> There was an old woman,
> Sold puddings and pies;
> Bursting with plump figs
> And dead currant flies.

The customary fare was not confined to Blackburn, being found in many other Lancashire and Yorkshire towns, but in some places it was eaten on the fifth or sixth Sunday in Lent. Few figs are harvested in England nowadays as they often prove difficult to ripen. This recipe calls for dried figs, which should be soaked overnight before use. It can of course be made with fresh ones if available, in which case they should be stewed until tender.

Fig or Fag Pie   (Serves 4–6)

8oz (225g) dried figs
Water to cover
1 level tbsp cornflour
2 tbsp brown sugar
1tsp mixed spice
1tbsp currants
8oz (225g) shortcrust pastry
Milk

Soak the figs in water overnight. Roll out the pastry and line a pie plate about 8in in diameter. Cover with foil and bake blind at 400°F (200°C; Gas mark 6) for about 20min. Meanwhile, drain the figs, reserving the juice, cut off the hard stalks and chop into quarters. Blend the cornflour with 1tbsp of the fig juice. Heat the rest of the fig juice with the sugar, spice and currants in a saucepan. Stir in the blended cornflour to thicken, and add the chopped figs. Bring to the boil and simmer for a minute or so to reduce a little. Take the half-baked pastry shell from the oven, remove foil, and spoon on the figs in their syrupy sauce. Brush pastry rim with milk. Return to oven for another 20min or until the pastry is browned.

> I heard a sound of scraping tripe,
> And putting apples wondrous ripe. . . .
> (Robert Browning, 1812–89, in 'The Pied Piper of
> Hamelin')

In the mid-nineteenth century, dishes of tripe, which is actually the inner lining of a cow's stomach, became fashionable in London eating places with connoisseurs making quite a fuss about them. ' "It's a stew of tripe", said the landlord smacking his lips,' wrote Dickens in *The Old Curiosity Shop*. Although it is possible to buy dressed tripe (soaked and partially cooked tripe) in most places, one must go to Lancashire to see large quantities of it being appreciated. The delicacy, as many claim it to be, was readily available in Blackburn when I last visited the town, and a favourite local recipe is as follows.

Tripe and Onions   (Serves 2)

1lb (450g) dressed tripe
8oz (225g) baby onions, or big ones sliced
1 pint (560ml) milk
2oz (56g) margarine
1 rounded tbsp flour
½tsp nutmeg
Salt and pepper

Wash and skin the onions. Simmer them with the tripe in the milk for an hour, or until tender. In another pan melt the margarine and stir in the flour to make a roux. Gradually add the milk that the tripe has been boiling in and stir to make a sauce. Add the nutmeg and season to taste. Simmer for a few minutes to thicken a bit, stirring continuously to stop it from sticking. Add the tripe and onions and simmer for another minute. Serve immediately with piles of mashed potatoes.

BLACKLEY

Election/'In' and 'Out' Muffins

A small modern bakery in Victoria Avenue, Blackley, Manchester is managed by two very enterprising brothers, Bill and Sam Ward. A few years ago, Bill came up with the idea of baking coloured muffins for the local municipal elections – blue for Conservative; red for Labour; and yellow for Liberal – and by the number of each colour muffin sold, he was able to predict accurately the election results. As a result of the success of the first venture, the election muffins are now made for all local and general elections, and are frequently featured on television and in the press. The same idea was applied to the Common Market referendum in 1975 when 'in' and 'out' muffins successfully forecast Britain's entry into Europe.

The colouring used for the election muffins is a vegetable dye – similar to that used for coloured cake-icing – and the recipe is the one normally used in the Ward bakery for muffins. The Ward brothers are also responsible for the Manchester Cob (see the Manchester section).

BLACKPOOL

Rock

Blackpool in Lancashire is the most famous seaside town in the north of England and is noted for its Tower, its autumn illuminations and its foremost confection – Blackpool rock. One of several Blackpool rock manufacturers is the Coronation Rock Company Ltd whose director, Mr P. D. Wilcock, kindly described rock making to me.

It is difficult to ascertain the exact origin of Blackpool rock, but it is believed to have been first made in east Lancashire in the nineteenth century. The rock is made by boiling sugar and glucose (in a ratio of two parts sugar to one part glucose) in large copper pans to 300°F (150°C). It is then poured onto a hot metal plate. 'The batch of toffee [says Mr Wilcock] is divided into parts – some to form the letters, usually red, some for the casing, in the case of the original Blackpool rock coloured pink, some for the crispy, crunchy interior which gives the finished product its brittleness.' The latter is aerated and flavoured with oil of peppermint, and red letters are built up in long strips. A whole batch weighing some 1¼cwt is made into a huge stick of rock and rolled on a batch roller machine. When the rock has cooled sufficiently, it is sized up and finally wrapped by hand since no machine has yet been invented to wrap the rock satisfactorily.

As well as the traditional lettered rocks, the Coronation Rock Company make 'Fruits, Lollipops, Fruit Rock and small Fruit Rock Pieces'.

BRISTOL

Bristol Cream and Milk

As most people are aware, Bristol Cream and Milk are nothing to do with dairy products but are celebrated sherries. These drinks (although entirely Spanish in origin) are sold by a British company, John Harvey & Sons Ltd, which was founded in 1796 in Bristol, a major wine port for many centuries. The origin of the name 'Bristol Cream' is said to have been unwittingly supplied by an aristocratic lady who toured the company's cellars some ninety years ago. After tasting the traditional Bristol Milk, she was invited by John Harvey II to sample a richer, albeit less popular blend of sherry. 'If that be Milk, then this is Cream', she is alleged to have enthused. And from then onwards, the richer sherry was marketed under the name Cream. The Harveys Wine Museum in Denmark Street, Bristol, is open to the public and houses a fascinating collection of items connected with sherry.

BUCKINGHAMSHIRE

Once upon a time, Buckinghamshire was famous for the cherries which grew in profusion in every village. There were numerous cherry jingles and each village had its own. Flackwell Heath's ran:

> Flackwell Heath? What do you think?
> Where cherries grow as black as ink!

Alas, the cherry orchards seem to have dwindled, and gone too is the Cherry Pie Feast which was held at the end of the summer. The cherry pies were like rather large pastry turnovers encasing the dark cherries in red, syrupy sauce, and in some parts of the county were called cherry bumpers. It is worth reviving this recipe, especially as it need no longer be seasonal – in the absence of fresh cherries, tinned cherry pie filling can be used. However, the old recipe below describes how the bumpers are made with fresh cherries.

Cherry Bumpers (Makes 4–5)

8oz (225g) shortcrust pastry
12oz (337g) cherries
2tbsp brown sugar
Milk
Caster sugar

Wash, stalk and stone the cherries and sprinkle with brown sugar. Roll out the pastry to about ½in thick and, using a saucer, cut as many circles as possible. Put a generous heap of the cherries on half of each circle, leaving the edges clear. Brush the edges with water, and fold the other half of the pastry over to make a turnover. Pinch the edges to seal, and mark the tops with a fork. Brush with milk and sprinkle with caster sugar. Bake for about 25min in an oven pre-heated to 400°F (200°C; Gas mark 6). A pint of beer was the traditional accompaniment for the bumpers at the Cherry Pie Feasts.

Rarebit

Buckinghamshire is also responsible for a jazzed-up version of the Welsh Rarebit (see Welsh section). A Bucks Rarebit was probably invented by someone unable to decide whether to have cheese or egg on toast, who finally had both at once. It is simply Welsh Rarebit topped with one or two poached eggs.

BURTON–UPON–TRENT

Beer

Burton-upon-Trent is renowned for its beery smell – with at least three main breweries and several smaller concerns this is inevitable! Some people love the pong, others hate it. Beer brewing started in the town in the thirteenth century when an unknown monk discovered that a most acceptable beverage could be brewed using water from the local wells, and barley from farmlands surrounding the Abbey. Little is chronicled about the enterprising monk – the town remembers more clearly Michael Bass of the famous brewing firm, who became Lord Burton under Gladstone's government, and who was responsible for the Town Hall and many other public buildings.

BURY

It has become fashionable to think of the simnel cake as an Easter speciality. Invariably a dark, rich, fruity affair, with two layers of marzipan, it is generally decorated with marzipan balls and fluffy yellow chicks. However, the simnel cake was originally concocted for Mothering Sunday or mid-Lent Sunday, when a slight lapse in the austere Lenten fast was permissible. This was the one day in the year when the older children, working away from home in domestic service, were allowed time off to return home and possibly attend their mother church with the rest of the family as was customary on this day. Thus a large cake was needed to feed the visiting offspring, and often other relatives as well.

The name simnel, so many claim, is derived from the Latin for flour, *similia*, but other authorities attribute the special cakes to the baker father of Lambert Simnel, pretender to the throne during Henry VII's reign. This suggestion is unlikely to be true as simnels were common long before this period. They are in fact mentioned in the Annals of the Church of Winchester for the year 1042. A declaration made by King Edward specified that whenever His Highness, or successors, donned their crowns at either Winchester, Westminster or Worcester, the convent of the city would be entitled to receive 100 simnels and a measure of wine.

In Bury it was common practice to start baking simnel cakes shortly after Christmas, as some slices were invariably sent to relatives overseas. One of the largest simnels ever made was baked by 'The Friends of Free Trade' in 1844, and was presented to the Anti-Corn League. It was about 1yd in diameter, 3in thick, and weighed 100lb. Even a recipe in a YMCA bazaar book of 1907 calls for '8 lbs. fine flour, 8 lbs. currants, 4 lbs. cut sultana raisins, 4 lbs. sugar, 3 lbs. butter, the water to be pressed out, 1 lb. candid peel, ½ lb. citron, 2 lbs. almonds, 2 ozs. nutmeg, cinnamon spice mixed, 16 new laid eggs, the rind of 3 lemons, finely grated, 1 lb. barm and a little baking powder'.

Traditionally, the Bury simnel is akin to a curranty bread, being round in shape and somewhat plain looking unlike the marzipan bedecked variety. It is however quite delicious and this recipe is more suitable for today's small families.

Bury Simnel Cake

1lb (450g) self-raising flour
3oz (84g) butter
3oz (84g) lard
1tsp cinnamon
1 tsp nutmeg
10oz (280g) sugar
1lb (450g) currants
4oz (112g) candied peel
4oz (112g) ground almonds
2 large eggs

Grease a large baking tray and dust with flour. Rub the butter and lard into the flour until the mixture resembles breadcrumbs. Mix the spices with the sugar and add to the fat and flour along with the currants, peel and almonds. Stir until well mixed. Add the eggs, which should be fork-mixed but not beaten, to make a very stiff dough. Add a little milk if really necessary, perhaps if the eggs are small. Remember though that the cake has to retain its own shape as it is not baked in a tin. Shape the dough into a round blob and put on the prepared tray. Bake in an oven preheated to 350°F (180°C; Gas mark 4) for an hour or so. The exact time varies depending on how much the dough spreads, so have a peep after an hour and continue baking until a knife comes out clean.

Black Pudding

Bury Black Pudding is another recipe associated with this Lancashire town. No one knows for certain when black puddings were first made in the area but Casewell's black pudding shop in Union Street traded from around 1810 to 1968. The recipe for Casewell's puddings remains a secret – one of the last owners, Mr Vincent Ashworth, claimed that it was the oldest known and had not been altered at all.

Another early black-pudding maker was a brawny Lancashire wrestler, Joshua Thompson, who started a business in 1865. His descendants, who took over the concern, claimed that Joshua was actually the inventor of the puddings. Joshua's great-grandson, Harry Reddish, who died in 1971 after fifty years in the black pudding trade, once hinted that his black puddings were made from pig's blood, seasoning, fat and spices encased in the skin from a cow's innards. Apparently the normal sheep innard skins, as used for restraining sausages, are far too tender for black puddings. Mr Reddish believed that the success of good puddings was in the mixing, the secret method of which he never revealed. He made on average half a ton of black pudding every week.

In 1965, the Minister of Agriculture proposed to establish a minimum meat percentage in black puddings, but as the Bury varieties do not contain any meat at all, only fat, they were not affected.

A Bury black pudding farm was featured on television in 1964. Many viewers were quite amazed to see farmer William Smith and his family 'harvest' black puddings from their farm in Whitefield. However, they had been specially planted for 1 April and viewers who telephoned the television studios to check their sanity were gently reminded of the date!

CAERPHILLY

Cheese

The mid-Glamorgan town of Caerphilly is celebrated for its Castle and its cheese. The Castle has the unique 'Leaning Tower of Caerphilly'; the remains of one of the Castle's drum towers deliberately blown up during the Civil War, in the seventeenth century, it is 13ft out of perpendicular and a fascinating spectacle to view. The Castle is the largest in Wales and the second largest in Britain.

Caerphilly Cheese is especially suitable for underground workers' digestions; the mild, clean flavour does not repeat when they bend. Thus it was a great favourite with the town's miners in earlier years, and earned itself a good reputation. However, of late, the production of the cheese within the town has virtually ceased, and it is now made in several western counties by large creameries. This white cheese matures within two weeks, and is best eaten in its natural state, in sandwiches, salads, etc, as it does not cook particularly well.

CALDER VALLEY

Greenery, by the name of *Polygonum bistorta*, which grows around the Calder Valley area in Yorkshire, is responsible for the local Dock Pudding. The spinach-like dish is akin to the Easterledge pudding from Westmorland, but few people outside these areas find this type of pudding very appealing. However the Calderites relish theirs, claim it is an excellent spring tonic, and eat it fried with bacon and potatoes for breakfast or supper.

Dock Pudding Championship takes place at the Calder Valley Arts Festival and recently attracted nearly fifty contestants.

Dock Pudding

2 pints sweet dock leaves (Polygonum bistorta)
1 handful young nettle tops

2 spring onions, chopped
Salt and pepper
1 good handful oatmeal
2oz (56g) butter

Clean and string the dock leaves and nettles, and boil them with the chopped onions in a little water, until tender. Season to taste and sprinkle in the oatmeal. Boil and stir for 10min. Finally, add the butter and leave to cool. Fry spoonfuls of the mixture in bacon fat, alongside the breakfast bacon.

CAMBRIDGE

The university city of Cambridge is crammed with book-shops, and overrun with bicycles – one feels quite out of place in a car! But a drive, cycle ride or simple stroll down narrow Trinity Street will lead you to Trinity College, where so many eminent personalities have received their education. It is in fact thanks to one of that college's undergraduates in the last century that we have the delicious, extravagant recipe, Crème Brulée. The scholar brought the recipe to Cambridge, having previously sampled it in Aberdeen, and offered it to the kitchens at Trinity College. Foolishly, the chef was not impressed and rejected the young student's recipe. Then, in 1879, the undergraduate became a Fellow of the college, and once more pressed the chef to sample his recipe. The result was an outstanding success, demolished with relish, and to this day, this dish is popular with scholars.

Although it is correctly named Crème Brulée, it is also known as Cambridge Cream, Caramel Cream, or Burnt Cream. The ingredients are few but great care is needed in the preparation or else Curdled Cream is unfailingly obtained. A tray of ice cubes is needed in the last stage of the recipe.

Crème Brulée   (6 servings)

6 egg yolks
8oz (225g) caster sugar
1 pint (560ml) single cream

Using a fork mix the egg yolks with a level tablespoon of the sugar in a bowl. Pour the cream into a pan, bring to the boil, and pour over the egg yolks in the bowl. It is now advisable to transfer the mixture to a double saucepan, or to balance the bowl over a pan of hot water, because on no account must the mixture be allowed to boil at this stage. Heat the mixture very gently until it thickens and coats the back of a spoon. Pour the mixture into a fireproof dish and bake in a slow oven at 300°F (150°C; Gas mark 2), until set. Leave to cool. Place layers of ice cubes in a larger dish and turn the grill on full. Sprinkle the sugar to form a thick layer on top of the cooled cream, and stand the dish containing the cream in the larger dish surrounding it with ice. This is necessary to prevent the heat from curdling the cream. Place under the hot grill and let the sugar caramelise. Serve cold.

CHEDDAR

Cheese

A drive through the magnificent Cheddar Gorge, with its awesome 450ft cliffs, is a bewilderingly beautiful experience. But avoid the high holiday season when traffic jams abound. Having travelled through the jagged, rugged, almost 'TV western' scenery, you will find the small Somerset town of Cheddar. There is much for the tourist to see; the caves of Gough and Cox, creepy yet wondrous, and bursting with splendid stalagmites and stalactites, the vintage motor museum, the old Market Cross and an old cheese press in somebody's garden. The energetic can clamber up all 322 steps – I think – of Jacob's Ladder for a better view of the surrounding countryside. There are dozens of little shops, many of them selling rounds, of varying sizes, of the traditional farmhouse Cheddar cheese.

It was probably first made sometime in the twelfth century, and some of the early cheeses were huge, often weighing over a hundredweight. The cheese is now the most popular of the English varieties, and is imitated, sometimes dreadfully, all over the world. Sadly, cheese-making is no longer practised in Cheddar itself, but the cheese sold in the town is made locally on farms in Somerset and neighbouring counties. It tastes much better than the plastic-wrapped Cheddar-type cheese oblongs in supermarkets. My especial favourite is the matured Cheddar 2lb round, clothed in grey, dingy-looking muslin – the cheese inside is divine! There are recipes for making a Cheddar-type cheese at home, but as most start 'take 6gal of milk from 3 consecutive milkings' and not many of you will have cows, I think I will omit that one. Instead, try this recipe for Cheddar Cheese Straws, which incidentally, are still made in Cheddar.

Cheese Straws

4oz (112g) plain flour
1 level tsp mustard powder
Pinch of salt

3oz (84g) butter
3oz (84g) Cheddar cheese
1 egg, separated

Sieve the flour with the mustard powder and salt. Rub in the butter to make a breadcrumb mixture. Grate in the Cheddar cheese (which can be old and dry) and mix well. Add the egg yolk and just enough of the white to bind the ingredients together. Turn on to a floured board and roll out to about ¼in. Cut into sticks about 4in × ½in and put on a non-stick baking tray. Rather than continuing to roll the trimmings, make them into walnut-size balls, and bake with the straws. Brush with the leftover egg white and bake in an oven preheated to 400°F (200°C; Gas mark 6) for 10min, or until golden-brown.

CHELSEA

There's a charm in the sound which nobody shuns,
Of 'smoking hot, piping hot, Chelsea buns!'

The Chelsea Bun was a way of life in the eighteenth and early nineteenth centuries, and the Old Bunn House – first mentioned by Dean Swift in his *Journal to Stella* (1712) – was one of London's most famous buildings. It stood in Pimlico, just outside Chelsea, and was patronised by royalty as well as many Londoners. It is said that both George II and George III were enthusiastic bun eaters. On one Good Friday in the early part of the nineteenth century, nearly a quarter of a million buns were demolished.

A replica of the Old Bunn House was erected in Sloane Square, London, for the Festival of Britain in 1951 and attracted much attention. Buns, made especially for the occasion from an old recipe, were eagerly consumed.

There is considerable uncertainty about the original Chelsea Bun recipe but Reginald Blunt, in a letter to *The*

Times in 1928, described one 200 year old version: 'they [the buns] were very rich and full of butter. They were square in shape and were made with eggs, with sugar, rind of lemon and spice, but without fruit.' The omission of fruit is a little strange since all present-day recipes call for currants.

Chelsea Buns   (Makes about 16)

THE DOUGH
7 fluid oz warm milk
½oz (14g) fresh yeast
1lb (450g) plain flour, strong white
1 level tsp salt
2oz (56g) butter
2½oz (70g) sugar
2 standard eggs

FILLING
1½oz (42g) butter
2oz (56g) sugar
2 level tsp mixed spice
3oz (84g) currants
1oz (28g) chopped candied peel

SUGAR GLAZE
1oz (28g) sugar
2 fluid oz milk

Cream the fresh yeast with a tablespoon of the 'hand-hot' milk. Sift the flour and salt together, and rub in the butter until the mixture resembles breadcrumbs. Beat the eggs with the sugar and stir into the mixture. Make a well in the centre and pour in the creamed yeast and remaining milk. Stir to make a soft dough. Cover the bowl with an oiled polythene sheet, and leave in a warm place, to double in size – about 45min. Turn onto a floured board and knead for a few minutes. Roll out the dough to make an oblong, roughly 20in × 16in. Melt the butter over a low heat and brush over the dough. Mix all the remaining filling ingredients and sprinkle over. Roll the oblong up, in a swiss roll fashion, and cut off 1in slices. Arrange on a baking tray, cut sides flat, with a slight space between each bun. Leave to prove for another 30min, or until the buns just nudge each other. Bake at 375°F (190°C; Gas mark 5) for 25–30min. Remove from oven and brush with sugar and milk glaze. Return to oven for another 3min.

CHESHIRE

Cheese

'To grin like a Cheshire cat', is a much-loved saying. Although the phrase's origin is not agreed by all, some believe that it came about because the tops of Cheshire cheeses were marked with the face of a cat. Lewis Carroll elaborated on the theme when he introduced Alice to that infuriating cat. 'It [the Cheshire Cat] vanished quite slowly, beginning with the end of the tail, and ending with the grin, which remained sometime after the rest of it had gone.'

Cheshire cheese is patriotically made in red, white and blue, and it is claimed that it is the oldest of all English cheeses. Described in the seventeenth century by the naval commander, Sir Kenelme Digby, in his *Closet Opened* as 'a quick, fat, rich and well-tasted cheese', it is made from milk from cows who graze on Cheshire's, and neighbouring Shropshire's, hills and dales. Basically a white cheese, it is crumbly, slightly salty, and silky-textured. Some people enjoy eating it with a slice of fruit cake.

The red is coloured with annatto, a natural colouring – although originally carrot juice was used – which gives the cheese the characteristic warm colouring without impairing the Cheshire flavour. The blue is unique since it is only produced by accident; it has to catch a certain mould which cannot be artificially injected. This latter variety is much praised by gourmets, but not so by the local folk in the old days. They used to employ the accidentally made blue cheese as a dressing for wounds. This is not as crazy as it sounds: it is only in comparatively recent years that the properties of penicillin have been understood and medicinally used. The old blue cheese contained penicillin.

Cheshire cheese is clearly represented in London's Fleet Street where a pub named The Cheshire Cheese has stood for many years. More about this London landmark can be found in the London section.

Salt

Cheshire salts are manufactured by slowly evaporating Cheshire brine, using the open pan process. They are all completely free from chemical and artificial additives and are popular for this reason. Several varieties of salt are produced ranging from natural culinary salts to bath salts and water softening salts for dishwashing machines. Natural crystal salt is especially suitable for table salt mills and grinders. Salt has been mined and prepared from the Northwich Cheshire area since Roman times, and the sole manufacturers are Ingram Thompson & Son Ltd, Lion Salt Works, Marston, Northwich, Cheshire. This long established company would always be pleased to give the addresses of local stockists to enquirers but for those in London, Harrods, Robert Jackson and Selfridges, stock this product.

CHORLEY

The Lancashire town of Chorley has to compete with nearby Eccles for cake sales. Chorley cakes are nowhere near so famous as the Eccles variety, but all the same, are worthy of note. They are made by a number of small bakers in the town and are also manufactured by several larger firms. One of the latter that I contacted, admitted that they had only recently introduced Chorley cakes into their production. Thus, opposing the general decline of many regional recipes, these cakes appear to be increasing in appeal.

Chorley Cakes (Makes 4–5)

8oz (225g) shortcrust pastry
4oz (112g) currants
1oz (28g) chopped, candied peel
2oz (56g) butter
2oz (56g) sugar
2tsp cinnamon
Milk for glazing

Grease a large baking sheet. Mix the sugar and cinnamon together and leave on one side. Roll out the pastry and cut circles using a plate with a 6in diameter. Melt the butter in a pan over a low heat, and mix in the dried fruit. Allow to cool for a minute and then put 1tbsp of the currant mixture in the middle of each pastry circle. Sprinkle generously with sugar and cinnamon. Brush round the edge of each circle with milk and gather up to enclose the fruit. Turn over and flatten with a rolling pin to make a cake about 4in in diameter. Make 4 cuts with a knife in the top, and brush with milk. Put on prepared tray and bake at 425°F (220°C; Gas mark 7) until golden brown – about 20min. They can be spread with butter before serving but are quite acceptable as they are.

COLCHESTER

Oysters

Colchester oysters were famous in Roman times. In fact the Romans enjoyed them so much, they took some back to Rome, probably slung in nets over the sides of their ships. This is verified by the finding of distinct River Colne oyster shells in ruins in Rome. According to the Roman historian, Pliny, 'the only good thing about England is its oysters'. That ancient quote is open to dispute, but the oysters known as 'Colchesters', certainly enjoyed worldwide recognition, and still do so today.

In 1181 the Borough of Colchester was granted the fishing

rights in the Colne, by a charter from Richard I. In return, the king received money which was supposed to help build Dover Castle, but more likely, financed another crusade. The fishery was then rented from the town by several different people until 1870, when local freeman of the river formed themselves into a company.

The reigning Colchester Fishery Ltd was founded in 1965. In their first year a mere 3,000 oysters were produced but recently, a million is a more accurate annual total. The season commences in early September when the Mayor, and others closely associated with the industry, go by boat to the Pyefleet Creek, where the oyster fattening-beds are found. The Mayor proceeds to make the first ceremonial dredge, the season is declared open, and light refreshments follow. In October, the famous Colchester Oyster Feast takes place in the town's Moot Hall.

The unsqueamish prefer to tackle their oysters fresh, alive and kicking from the half shell, and feel them wriggling down their innards (so I have been told). These brave souls will not require this recipe which offers a more genteel way to eat oysters. To open an oyster, which incidentally should be discarded if not tightly closed, lay it on a non-slip surface, with the flat shell uppermost. Holding it firmly, insert the point of a knife in the shell's hinge, and wiggle it about until you feel it 'give'. Open the shell, cut the muscle cleanly away, and reserve its liquor.

Oyster Fritters

10 oysters
Salt and pepper
BATTER
4oz (112g) flour
Pinch of salt
1 egg, separated
½ pint (280ml) milk, approx

Remove the oysters from their shells, as previously described. Season with salt and pepper and boil in their liquor until the edges begin to curl. Make the batter. Mix the flour, salt, egg yolk, and enough of the milk to make a batter thick enough to coat the back of the spoon. Whisk the egg white and fold into the batter just prior to using. Heat some oil in a deep saucepan until nearly smoking. Dip the oysters in the batter, then immerse them in the hot oil and fry until crisp and brown. A chip basket simplifies the operation. Serve immediately with lemon wedges and brown bread and butter.

CORNWALL

Cornwall is a land practically surrounded by water – the sea and the River Tamar – and is full of magic and superstition. It is often called the Land of Merlin after the legendary wizard. Many ancient traditions, some originating in pagan rites, are still upheld: the Hurling of the Silver Ball at St Ives, the Helston Furry Dance, and the Marhamchurch Revel all entertain the visitor and are important events for the Cornish folk. Bonfires are also favoured in Cornwall and a whole chain of them are lit on Midsummer Day's eve to ward off bad spirits and protect cattle from disease.

A Cornish Pasty seems originally to have been a kind of pastry turnover containing many different fillings. In the old days they were usually pretty substantial affairs, devised to fill a hungry farm worker at lunchtime, and contained a full dinner within their enveloping crusts – some hefty examples measured up to a foot in length! Miners liked pasties because they were convenient and the more modest concoctions could be carried in their pockets. Some farmers' wives stuck pastry initials on one end of the pasty. The eater commenced at the opposite end and if his meal was interrupted, causing him to put down his precious pasty, no one else could steal a couple of bites without discovery.

Nowadays, unfortunately, many Cornish pasties contain little but a few lumps of gristle and mushy potato, not a very appetising object. However, the list of more commendable fillings is endless and every Cornishman has his favourite. There is even a saying that the Devil would never dare to cross the Tamar and venture into Cornwall, for fear of his flesh ending up in a pasty.

> Pastry rolled out like a plate,
> Piled with turmut, tates and mate,
> Doubled up and baked like fate
> That's a Cornish pasty.
>
> (Trad)

Cornish Pasties (Makes 4)

1lb (450g) shortcrust pastry
12oz (337g) chuck steak, cubed small
4oz (112g) liver, chopped
2 medium potatoes, peeled and chopped
1 large onion, skinned and chopped
Salt and pepper
Milk for glaze

Roll the pastry out and cut into 8in rounds using a plate as a guide. Mix all the other ingredients in a bowl. Divide equally between the pastry rounds, piling the mixture on one half of each round only. Brush round the rims with water and fold the uncovered halves over the meat mixture, turnover style, and pinch the edges to seal. Make a few slits for the steam to escape. Brush with milk and bake in an oven at 400°F (200°C; Gas mark 6) for 15min. Then reduce heat to 350°F (180°C; Gas mark 4) and bake for a further 45min, or until the meat is tender. Cover with foil if they start to brown too much. They can be eaten hot at the dinner table or cold on a picnic, but not, I would advise, carried in one's pocket!

When the first Cornish Pasty was made is anyone's guess but it has been suggested that the shape of the pasty is reminiscent of a quarter moon with blunted horns. This being the emblem of Astarte, the goddess of the Phoenicians who came to Cornwall to trade in tin, it is possible that they may have introduced some similar food.

Cornish Hoggins

Hoggins are made from the same ingredients as pasties but the filling is heaped in the middle of each pastry round, and the edges are drawn up and sealed on top.

It is probably due to the presence of the tin mines, once very important in Cornwall, that we have the recipe for Saffron Cake. It is generally believed that the ancient Phoenicians offered spices, saffron included, in exchange for Cornish tin. The use of these spices in cooking soon spread all over England, and saffron was cultivated in many places including Saffron Walden (saffron fields) in Essex. However, nowadays Cornwall seems to be one of the few places in England where saffron is still used in the kitchen. The strong yellow spice is actually a powder obtained from a variety of crocus, and is generally available from chemists or some supermarkets.

Saffron Cake

¼–½tsp powdered saffron
¼ pint (140ml) boiling water
¼ pint (140ml) warm milk
½oz (14g) dried yeast
½ level tbsp sugar
1lb (450g) plain flour
Pinch of salt
4oz (112g) margarine
4oz (112g) lard
2oz (56g) sugar

6oz (168g) currants
2oz (56g) sultanas
1oz (28g) mixed, candied peel

Put the saffron in a small bowl and pour the boiling water over. Leave for at least 6hr, or overnight, to infuse. Mix the yeast into half of the milk with ½ level tbsp of sugar. Leave for 15min to froth. Sieve the flour and salt and rub in the margarine and lard until the mixture resembles bread-crumbs. Stir in the sugar, currants, sultanas and peel, and make a well in the middle. Pour in the saffron water, the activated yeast liquid and enough of the remaining milk to mix into a soft dough. Cover with an oiled polythene sheet and leave in a warm place to double in size. Grease either a 2lb loaf tin or an 8in round cake tin and line with grease-proof paper. Turn the risen dough onto a floured board and knead to exclude any air bubbles. Put into the prepared tin and leave to prove again, about 30min. Bake in a preheated oven at 350°F (180°C; Gas mark 4) for 1¼hr. Test with a skewer to ensure that it is sufficiently baked.

From cake to fish. Many years ago pilchard fishing was a very prosperous industry in Cornwall, but of late it has practically ceased. In England, we now import pilchards from abroad, whereas once upon a time we were enterprising enough to export large numbers to the Mediterranean. It is thanks to the large quantity of pilchards that were sent from Cornwall to Italy that we have the following rhyme.

> Here's health to the Pope—
>   May he never know sorrow,
> With pilchards today,
>   And pilchards tomorrow.

Cornish cooks used to simmer potatoes and pilchards in cream, the result being known as Dippy. Star Gazy Pie is another traditional pilchard dish – to be approached with care if you view fish heads with dismay. If you really cannot face eight pairs of eyes watching you while you guzzle the owners' bodies, you would be well advised to discard the heads along with the backbones.

Star Gazy Pie   (Serves 3–4)

8 pilchards (or 4 herrings could be used)
Salt and pepper
Little chopped parsley
2tbsp breadcrumbs
2 large eggs
1tbsp tarragon vinegar
3 slices streaky bacon
8oz (225g) shortcrust pastry
Milk

Clean, scale and bone the fish, and keep the heads on one side. Roll the fish up and put in a buttered pie dish. Season with salt, pepper and parsley, and sprinkle the breadcrumbs over. Beat the eggs with the vinegar and pour over. Lay the bacon on top. Roll out the pastry to make a lid to fit your pie dish, and fit it on. Make 8 (or 4) slots in the pastry and wedge a fish head in each. (In some old recipes the fish are actually baked whole, standing on their tails, but this makes the pie very messy to eat. And anyway, the fish do not find it so easy to balance on their tails – at least mine do not!). Brush the pastry with milk and bake in an oven at 350°F (180°C; Gas mark 4) for 50–55min.

Mahogany

A favourite drink with Cornish fishermen was known as Mahogany. It consists of one cup of treacle beaten with two cups of gin, presumably to be shared by several people. It is said to have been an ideal drink to accompany pilchards or 'fair-maids' as they were affectionately known. This local name was perhaps a corruption of *fumade* (Spanish for smoking) as many Spanish finishing boats used to anchor off the Cornish coast, and smoke some of their catch for eating.

On 24 August, which is St Bartholomew's Day, an interesting custom is observed in Gulval where years ago mead brewing was commonplace, as it was in many other West Country villages. St Bartholomew is the patron saint of honey-makers and bee-keepers. Thus it is appropriate that this day be chosen for the Blessing of the Mead. (Mead, of course, contains a good percentage of honey.) First, a short service is held in the church. Then all the participants transfer to the Mead Hall where the vicar blesses the mead and traditionally pours it into the St Ives Loving Cup.

The following recipe is an updated version of an old

Cornish one and is similar to *metheglin* – or spiced mead – as it contains ginger as well as honey and water. There are many other Cornish recipes for mead, all varying slightly, but I found this one particularly good. Many of the ingredients needed to make mead can be purchased from wine-making shops. In the past, tannin had to be extracted from tea, and yeast in a handy, measured form was unheard of. Sometimes mead was served warm but this practice is not favoured today.

Cornish Mead

2oz (56g) Jamaican root ginger
3lb (1.280kg) light honey
7 pints (4l) water
Juice 2 lemons
¼tsp grape tannin
1 nutrient tablet
1oz (28g) (approx) yeast or enough to work it

Chop the ginger, bruise it and tie in a muslin bag. Stir the honey and water in a large pan, drop in the muslin bag and slowly bring to the boil. Spoon off any scum as soon as it rises to the surface. Remove from heat once boiling point has been reached. Cool to blood heat and add the remaining ingredients. Remove the ginger bag and pour the mead into a container with an air-lock. Leave in one position, in a constant temperature of 70°F (22°C) until fermentation is complete – the airing cupboard is usually suitable. Mead takes somewhat longer than ordinary wines to ferment but there is no way of hurrying it. Rack off, bottle and cork in the normal way, when it is completely clear. The longer you leave it before drinking it, the better it is – 12–24 months is usually specified. However, if you are impatient, it is drinkable after six months.

Cornish Mead Wine and Cornish Liqueur Mead are both produced by the Cornish Mead Co Ltd at the Meadery,

Newlyn, Cornwall, from recipes handed down through the centuries. It is believed that mead was drunk by the legendary King Arthur and the Knights of the Round Table when they gathered at Tintagel in North Cornwall, many centuries ago.

But whether you buy your mead or brew it yourself, remember the old Cornish toast when you sip the honey drink on New Year's Eve:

> A Happy New Year, and a young woman,
> And plenty of money with your wife!

COVENTRY

Coventry Godcakes are no longer available from bakers in Coventry. Did the terrible bombing that this Warwickshire city suffered in 1940 destroy as many customs as buildings? The city itself has recovered magnificently. The beautiful new Cathedral is a perfect blending of the old interspersed with modern lines, and the traffic-free shopping precinct was one of the first in the country. There is an old rhyme, similar to Banbury's:

> Ride a cock-horse to Coventry cross
> To see what Emma can buy,
> A penny white cake I'll buy for her sake,
> And a two-penny tart or a pie.

I could find no cross in Coventry but instead I admired the dominating statue of Lady Godiva, who tradition says rode through the streets naked to protest about the high taxes introduced by her own husband, Leofric, Earl of Mercia.

Returning to the less outrageous – Coventry Godcakes were traditionally given to godchildren by their respective godparents at Easter and the New Year. They were known to all classes, from the very poor to the extremely wealthy, but they varied in size according to the prosperity or otherwise of the giver. The cheapest godcakes cost one old halfpenny, and were hawked on the streets, whereas the larger ones cost, even in the mid-nineteenth century, up to £1. Their unusual triangular shape was said to represent the Holy Trinity.

Small greens at crossroads were also once known locally as godcakes.

Coventry Godcakes

MINCEMEAT FILLING
4oz (112g) butter
2tbsp sugar

8oz (225g) currants
4oz (112g) chopped, candied peel
2tsp mixed spice
1tsp cinnamon
1tbsp rum or rum flavouring

1lb (450g) puff pastry
1 egg white or milk
Caster sugar for sprinkling

Melt the butter in a saucepan and add all the other mince-meat filling ingredients. Stir over a low heat for a few minutes and then put on one side to cool. It cannot be used until the butter is quite cold. Roll out the pastry to about an ⅛in and cut into oblong shapes measuring about 6in × 8in. Put a generous spoonful of the mincemeat in the centre of each, and flatten a little with the back of a spoon. Fold the pastry over to make an elongated triangle shape, encasing the mincemeat and wetting and pinching the edges to secure. Turn over and make three slits in the top. Brush with egg white or milk and sprinkle liberally with sugar. Bake in an oven preheated to 400°F (200°C; Gas mark 6) for about 15min.

Relatively recent variations of these puff pastry cakes are the triangular jam puffs known in the bakery trade as 'Coventrys'. They are made in the same way as the godcakes, but instead of mincemeat, they are filled with raspberry jam.

CRASTER

Kippers

Craster is a coastal village in Northumberland well loved for its flavoursome kippers. Mr K. L. Robson of L. Robson & Sons Ltd, tells me that his smoking rooms are 100 years old, and he attributes the superiority of the Craster Kipper to the original method of pure oak smoking without chemicals or colouring. He uses the best quality herring available, and likes his own kippers simply grilled. The Robson curing house is open to the public, and from June to September one can view the whole fascinating procedure from start to finish.

CUMBERLAND

Cumbrians will try and tell you that they only cook good, plain food. Good and nourishing indeed it is, but plain? I hardly think so. Cumberland has lent its name to many culinary delights through the years – things have blossomed considerably from the days when oatmeal 'poddish' was the staple fare. Technically, the county of Cumberland no longer exists. Since April 1974, it has been merged with the other old county, Westmorland, to form Cumbria, but the old name persists as a prefix to many recipes.

Mutton Hams

Cumberland Sauce was probably first made to go with the old Cumberland mutton hams, which are quite rare these days. They are pickled with salt, brown sugar and juniper berries before they are finally smoked. The sauce is quite simple to make and turns any mutton ham or boiled bacon into a cordon bleu speciality.

Cumberland Sauce

1 large orange
1 lemon
4tbsp redcurrant jelly
½ teacup port, or red wine such as elderberry, damson, etc
1tbsp glacé cherries (optional)

Finely grate the orange and lemon rinds, being careful not to include any of the white pith, and simmer with the juice from the fruit for a minute or so. Add the redcurrant jelly and port or fruit wine, and stir until the jelly melts. Add the cherries, if liked, and simmer for a few minutes until the sauce thickens a little. Take to the table in a gravy boat, warm if hot gammon is being served, or cold with cold ham.

Christmas pudding would never be quite right without Cumberland Rum Butter but originally, it was spread on biscuits for guests at new babies' arrival celebrations. The baby was often given a spoonful of the butter and this was described as the infant's first taste of earthly food; the butter promised the baby the goodness of life; the rum, the spirit of life; the sugar, the sweetness of life; and the nutmeg, the spice of life. The rum butter was made in beautiful old china bowls but these were never cleaned completely of their contents at the baby celebrations – a little of the sticky rum butter was left in the bowl so that the coins thrown in it for the child adhered to the sides, symbolising that riches would always stick with the infant.

Cumberland Rum Butter

8oz (225g) butter
1lb (450g) moist, brown sugar
Pinch of cinnamon or nutmeg
½ teacup rum

Place the butter in a large, oven-proof bowl and put in an oven set to a very low temperature until it melts. Stir in the sugar and a good pinch of spice. Pour in the rum (and do be generous with it!) and beat thoroughly. Pour into a dish or several small pots and leave to harden.

According to local history, the Cumbrian use of rum came about because, years ago, rum smuggling was rife on this suitably rugged coastline, and local folk took 'accidentally broken' casks home with them rather than let the liquor drip to waste. Rum butter, so a fanciful tale goes, was first discovered by a little old lady whose dubiously acquired cask of rum leaked in her larder, soaking her sugar and butter stores.

Cumberland Sausage is one of those lengthy things coiled neatly like a ship's rope. The sausages are more expensive than ordinary ones because they contain no cereal or bulk, just minced pork and herbs. To make a Cumberland Sausage at home you really need a sausage-filler attachment, as to fill a long, continuous skin by hand is almost impossible. You can however roll the sausagemeat into a long length with floured hands, and then coil it in the Cumberland fashion. However, you will find that having no skin it tends to become a solid mass as it cooks. Nevertheless the recipe is worth trying even if you bake it like a sausagemeat cake.

Cumberland Sausage

2lb (900g) pork, lean and fat
½tsp salt
Pinch of black pepper
1 level tbsp sage, or mixed herbs

Mince the pork twice and work in the seasoning and herbs. The varieties of herbs for this recipe differ from butcher to butcher, but sage usually predominates. Fill a long length of sausage casing, if you have the necessary equipment, or take one of the courses of action described above. Bake the coiled sausage or sausagemeat cake in a buttered meat tin for about 15min at 400°F (200°C; Gas mark 6). Then carefully turn it over with a fish slice and bake for another 15min, or longer if you like your sausages well browned. Cumbrian housewives cut off varying lengths of the sausage according to appetites – say 8in for Dad and 4½in for little Willy – and serve with apple sauce. Of course if you have a large family to feed, you can make a larger sausage, perhaps several feet coiled to the size of a dinner plate.

DERBY

Cheese

Derby Cheese is one of the rarer English cheeses. So rare in fact that I was unable to buy the stuff in Derby. But to be fair it was just after Christmas, and apparently everyone stocks up with Derby Cheese for the festivities. The irony of the visit was that on my return home my mother had some of this elusive cheese in her refrigerator.

The first English cheese factory was established at Longford in Derbyshire in 1870, and in the same year the Derbyshire Cheese Factory Association was formed. This latter concern also established a second factory, converted from an old warehouse, in Derby, and the first cheese was produced there on 8 April 1870, but it is uncertain which variety was made.

Cheese-making had of course been thriving in farmhouses for centuries, but the Derbyshire factories made the first attempts at manufacturing large quantities of cheese under one roof. On old Derbyshire farms, the cutting of a newly matured cheese was a serious business, and all the family and farm-hands gathered to witness the ceremonial. The cheese was, after all, the result of many months' careful attention by the dairymaid – invariably the farmer's wife – during which time it had to be constantly observed and protected from cold draughts. Once everybody had visibly examined the cheese, they sat themselves around the heavily leaden dinner table to watch the master of the house, whose privilege it was to cut the huge round. Traditionally a large knife, rather than a wire, was used for Derby Cheese, so that its flaky grain was not spoilt. The dairymaid's toil was applauded if the cheese was deemed to have a smooth, mild flavour.

Derby Cheese is not unlike Cheddar, but it has a more buttery texture, and a characteristic subtle flavour. Sage Derby is an interesting cheese, with green blotches or stripes which are caused by the addition of sage. This herb was originally blended with the cheese curd many centuries ago for its medicinal virtues – it was claimed to be beneficial to the nerves and brain – as well as to vary the flavour.

DERBYSHIRE

In the seventeenth century, it is probable that oatcakes were the staple diet of many Derbyshire peasants – this being the only food many of them could afford. It was due to the high lime content of the soil that oats were grown in preference to wheat. About 14lb of oats are needed to produce 8lb of oatmeal, and the men who dealt in oatmeal were known as mealmen or swalers.

The ingredients for oatcakes, or havercakes as they were sometimes called, were mixed in a large wooden bowl, a doschen. As there was no brewer's yeast in early days, the bowl was left unwashed, and some of the previous mix adhered to the sides of the bowl and acted as a raising agent for the fresh batch. In very hot weather however, it was thought that the bowl itself was sour enough to raise the new mixture and so it was gently wiped 'clean'. The thick batter mixture was poured on a bakestone which had been lightly greased with bacon fat. The batter was coaxed to spread out with the back of a wooden ladle to make a cake anything up to 18in in diameter. According to some elderly Derbyshire farmers, large numbers of oatcakes were often made at once, and then hung up, as one hangs up the washing, in their farm kitchens. They were left there until they were fried for breakfast, or toasted for tea. Very poor folk ate the cakes 'raw' whereas the better off spread theirs with beef dripping, and more recently, with butter. In some parts, it was thought that the baking of oatcakes in a house would protect the building from witches.

The Charles Cotton Hotel, situated between Buxton and Ashbourne, two miles off the main road, still serves Derbyshire Oatcakes for breakfast. Mrs Willis, the proprietor, writes: 'They are the size of a dinner plate and one can toast and butter them, but the most popular way of serving them is with the breakfast bacon and eggs, etc, fried in bacon fat, a good hearty Derbyshire breakfast.' She adds that they are very popular, especially with guests from the south who have not eaten them before. The oatcakes can be obtained from many bakers, and even butchers, in the vicinity of the hotel. The recipe given here is a traditional one.

Derbyshire Oatcakes

1 pint (560ml) warm water
½oz (14g) fresh yeast
1 level tsp salt
8oz (225g) oatmeal
4oz (112g) wholemeal flour
2 level tsp baking powder

Crumble the fresh yeast into the warm (no hotter than blood heat) water. Mix the oatmeal, salt, flour and baking powder, and gradually pour in the yeast and water. Beat the mixture to a 'sawdusty' batter and leave in a warm place for 30min. Oil a large, heavy based frying pan or better still, a griddle pan, and place over a moderate heat. Pour a small cup of the batter into the hot pan. Tilt the pan to spread the mixture, or spread it with a spatula. Cook for about 4min on each side, and then an extra 2min on the first side. Transfer to a wire rack and let it steam for a few minutes. Keep warm until serving time, or alternatively allow to cool and toast, or fry with the breakfast bacon. If toasted, spread thickly with butter.

DEVON

Throughout the county there are many tea rooms, often in delightful beam and plaster establishments, and the famous cream teas are one of Devon's specialities. 'Clotted cream and new cream put together, is eaten more for a sensual appetite than for any good nourishment.' (Andrew Boorde 1542).

Clotted cream is really scalded milk. In the past farmers' wives used to scald their milk over peat fires as it was considered to give the cream rather a good flavour. Nowadays the clotted cream industry has become so commercialised that it is practically impossible to drive through Devon without being tempted to buy some, and you will perhaps even be persuaded to send some through the post to friends at home. Many firms, including Wattys Delicatessen, 16, Catherine Street, Exeter, Devon, accept orders by post.

With a little luck and patience, though, clotted cream can be made at home. Start with a small amount of milk, as the recipe describes, and increase the quantity as you become more proficient.

Clotted Cream

Pour 1 pint (560ml) of creamy milk (Jersey is fine) into a saucepan with a heavy base. Cover and leave undisturbed until the cream rises to the top. This takes about 12hr in the summer and up to 24hr in winter, but with central heating, adjustments to the time required have to be made! Lift the pan very gently onto the hob and heat on the lowest possible setting. Try not to jerk the pan at all as this will break up the cream. Leave to clot, making sure that it does not boil – this would be disastrous. When a solid ring forms round the edge and the surface looks all wrinkled, the cream is done. The time this takes varies according to the size and shape of the pan, the heat, etc, but the longer it takes, the better. Still moving the pan gently, transfer it to a cool place – the bottom of the refrigerator for instance – and leave for 24hr. Spoon the clotted cream into a separate dish and use as required.

Some energetic people beat the cream vigorously until it turns into butter. But be warned, churning is a time-consuming operation, as the old rhyme reminds us.

> Come, butter, come,
> Come, butter, come;
> Peter stands at the gate
> Waiting for a butter cake.
> Come, butter, come.

Personally, I would rather use the cream for splits or scones.

Devon Splits are little scones which were once called by different names in different parts of Devon. They varied a little in size and shape but basically Rounds, Chudleys, Tuffs, and Farthing and Hapenny Buns were all the same kind of thing.

Devon Splits (Makes 10)

8oz (225g) self-raising flour
Pinch of salt
3oz (84g) margarine
2oz (56g) caster sugar
Milk

Sift the flour with the salt and rub in the margarine until the mixture resembles breadcrumbs. Add the caster sugar and enough milk (about 3 or 4tbsp) to mix to a fairly stiff dough. Turn onto a floured board and knead until the dough no longer cracks. Roll out to about ½in thick and cut out 2½in rounds. Place on a greased baking tray and bake in an oven preheated to 400°F (200°C; Gas mark 6) for about 15min, when they should be well risen. Allow to cool and serve traditionally split – hence of course the name – with lashings of clotted cream and strawberry jam.

Devonshire Junket was once popular at the seaside villages and to go 'a-junketing' at the weekend was a special family treat. The junket was often served spread with clotted cream and sprinkled with nutmeg or cinnamon. In early days, the inner lining of a calf's stomach was used to set the milk. Nowadays, thank goodness, we are able to substitute bottled essence of rennet. Devon Junket is different from others, being flavoured with brandy, and looks most attractive made in a large china bowl.

Devon Junket   (Serves 4–6)

1 pint (560ml) milk
1tbsp sugar
1tbsp brandy
1tsp essence of rennet
Clotted cream and cinnamon or nutmeg to serve

Heat the milk in a saucepan to blood heat, ie, so that it feels neither hot nor cold. The milk must not boil, or have been boiled and allowed to cool, or else the junket will not set. Pour the milk into a serving bowl and stir in the sugar and brandy. Finally add the rennet which must be added after the flavourings. Leave the bowl undisturbed until the milk sets. Before serving, carefully spread with clotted cream, or whipped cream, and sprinkle with cinnamon or nutmeg.

Squab Pie is an ancient recipe which is often associated with Devon. However, the more recent recipes for this dish no longer call for the use of squabs (young pigeons) but instead suggest using lamb. Indeed pigeons are no longer a fashionable table bird, as they were in the last century; maybe we have grown rather too fond of the ever hungry birds in London's Trafalgar Square. Anyway, they have become increasingly expensive to acquire and thus it is feasible to presume that poorer families were the first to introduce Squab Pies made with mutton, possibly about fifty years ago.

Squab Pie   (Serves 4)

1lb (450g) cooking apples
2 medium onions
1lb (450g) neck of lamp chops
Salt and pepper
1 level tsp cinnamon
1 rounded tbsp sugar
¼ pint (140ml) cider, stock or water
12oz (337g) shortcrust pastry

Peel, core and slice the apples and skin and chop the onions. Put half of each into a pie dish to cover the base. Next arrange the chops on top and season well with salt, pepper and cinnamon. Top with the remaining apple and onion. Stir the sugar into the cider and pour over the dish. Roll out the pastry and make a cover to fit the dish. Flute the edges and use any pastry trimmings to make 'leaves' for decoration. Brush with milk and bake in an oven at 400°F (200°C; Gas mark 6) for ½hr. Then reduce the temperature to 325°F (170°C; Gas mark 3) and continue cooking for another 40min. It is advisable to lay a sheet of foil over the pastry after the first half hour, to prevent it becoming too browned. In the eighteenth century it was fashionable to pour 'clouted' cream, as they used to call it, over the pie before serving.

DONCASTER

Doncaster in South Yorkshire has long been associated with horse-racing and when Dickens went to the races there in 1857, he disapproved of the 'horse-mad, betting-mad, drunken-mad, vice-mad crowds'. It is a shame he did not sample some Doncaster Butterscotch – he might have formulated a better opinion of the town.

Doncaster Butterscotch and other old fashioned sweetmeats were sold by Mr Samuel Parkinson from 11 May 1817 onwards, at his shop at 50 and 51, High Street, Doncaster. Mr Parkinson was a most successful and enterprising businessman, and soon ventured out as a grocer and tea-trader as well. His son, William, went into his father's business, and duly took into partnership a Mr Parker following his father's death in 1870. Mr Parkinson possessed much of his father's enterprise and incited yet more fame, and more sales for the butterscotch, by persuading the newly opened steam companies to sell the sweet commodity in the railway waiting rooms. S. Parkinson & Son Ltd are now part of a large group of confectionery companies, but the old style butterscotch, in 4oz and 8oz packets (with the familiar beefeater emblem) is still made and is sold in sweetshops everywhere.

The name of butterscotch is not associated with Scotch whisky. It came about simply because the ingredients – the butter and sugar – were scotched or scorched.

Doncaster Butterscotch

1lb (450g) white sugar
½ pint (280ml) milk
6oz (168g) butter
Pinch of cream of tartar

Put the sugar and milk in a heavy based pan over a low heat and let the former dissolve slowly. Add the butter in small chunks, and when it has melted, stir in the cream of tartar. Bring to the boil and let it bubble until it reaches soft ball stage (240°F; 115°C) – a ball should form when a spoonful of the mixture is dropped in cold water, but it should flatten quite easily. Pour into oiled trays, and mark into squares before it sets too hard.

DORSET
Knobs

The small bakehouse, on the coastal road between Bridport and Lyme Regis in Dorset, has its doors open so that the public can see what is happening when baking is in progress. It is actually situated in the village of Morecombelake and is owned by the Moores family. You can watch Dorset Knobs being moulded by hand and then being put on rotating trays for their long, slow bake. The recipe for these unusual biscuits most probably dates from the seventeenth century, and has not really altered much through the years. Nowadays though, the knobs – somewhat similar in size to golf balls – are very slightly smaller than the early versions.

The Moores family was first connected with baking in the early nineteenth century, when they had a homestead farmhouse at Stoke Mills near the Dorset/Somerset border.

Wheat grown on the farm was ground in an old fashioned water mill and used to make bread and knob biscuits. Dorset Knobs were especially popular with farm workers who used to dip them in their early morning tea, and eat them for a quick breakfast before attending to their early morning milking duties. This practice is still carried on, but is rather thoughtless, I think, as poor Mr Moores goes to a great deal of trouble to ensure that his biscuits are very crisp!

Easter Biscuits

The bakery has been in its present position since the early 1920s and now makes about 20,000 biscuits a day. As well as the knobs, the establishment produces several other kinds of biscuits, including very good Easter Biscuits. These are about 4in in diameter, studded with currants, and according to Mr Moores, very popular. But not everything runs smoothly for bakers all the time, and crisp biscuits have a nasty habit of snapping. Thus, on a corner shelf in the adjoining shop, you will find a splendid bargain in the 'Moores Mistakes'. These broken biscuits, tasting just as good, remind one of the days when all the grocers had broken biscuits for sale.

On my way through Dorset, I stopped at the Admiral Hood, a typical country pub at Mosterton. Here I spied pickled eggs for sale at the bar, and was amused to learn that the locals eat these with a bag of crisps, calling the combination 'Chicken 'n Chips'.

Dorset Pickled Eggs

8 or 9 eggs
1½ pints (840ml) cider or white vinegar
Small piece stem ginger
Few peppercorns
1½oz (42g) pickling spice
1 cinnamon stick
Few cloves of garlic, skinned

Hardboil the eggs, remove the shells and put in a wide necked jar – an old pickle or coffee jar will be suitable. Boil the vinegar and spices, which incidentally can be varied to suit personal preferences, for about 8min. Then pour slowly over the eggs. Allow to cool slightly and screw the cap on. Leave to mature for a month before sampling, and do remember the crisps. Thereafter the eggs seem to keep indefinitely. If you plan to make a good supply, say treble the quantity given, scrounge a large, sweet jar from your local sweetshop.

DUBLIN

Dublin, the capital of the Republic of Ireland, nestles near the east coast, just north of the Wicklow Mountains. Basically it is a late Georgian city with a spattering of more ancient architecture, and the usual crop of modern buildings. A property in Capel Street housed James II's famous mint where the old brass coins were made. But perhaps the most famous product of Dublin is Guinness stout – the St James Gate brewery being founded in the city by Arthur Guinness in 1759. The brewery, much expanded, is still thriving today although the Gate itself has long been absent. More about Mr Guinness and his stout can be found in the Irish section.

Coddling means to many of us an old-fashioned method of soft-boiling eggs, but in Dublin a coddle is a tasty dish of a far more adventurous, if not exactly gastronomic, nature. It has been made for the last few centuries and is similar to that old faithful fish and chips in that it is eaten when the pubs turn out, on Saturday nights in particular. Originally it was made without potatoes but the more modern recipes all seem to include spuds. This surely is a grave mistake (there are plenty of Irish recipes using potatoes anyway) as they tend to weaken the dish by sopping up too much of the flavour. Thus an original recipe is given.

Dublin Coddle   (Serves 4–6)

1lb (450g) onions
8 rashers bacon
Salt and pepper
8 sausages (fat butcher's type not those skinny things)
Water

Peel and slice the onions and snip the bacon rashers into small pieces. Mix these in a saucepan and season well. Lay the sausages on top and add enough water to cover. Fold a double sheet of greaseproof paper over the top of the pan and put on the lid, making a rather tight fit. Simmer gently for 30–45min taking care not to let the mixture become too mushy. Serve with hunks of soda bread and wash down, if not already too sozzled, with plenty of stout.

Dublin Bay Prawns

In Dublin's fair city, where girls are so pretty,
I first set my eyes on sweet Molly Malone,
As she wheeled her wheelbarrow
Through streets broad and narrow,
Crying, Cockles and Mussels, alive, alive, oh!
(Anon)

Being so close to the sea, it is quite obvious that shellfish rank high on Dublin menus. But rather than cockles and mussels, it is the Dublin Bay prawn that has become notable. These prawns, the Irish claim, are larger and pinker than any other prawns. Their generous proportions are probably due to their not really being prawns at all, but a species of the Norway lobster. They were first called prawns by the fishermen who brought them to the streets of Dublin nearly two centuries ago, and the name has stuck. They are in season all year round but are at their best from March to September. Dublin Bay prawns can be used in the usual prawn cocktail or even fried in crispy batter, but their delicate, unique flavour is best sampled if they are steamed in a colander (not a plastic one) over a pan of simmering water for about 15min. This done, shell the little fish by pushing the tail towards the beady eye until the belly skin cracks, then pull off both ends. Sauté them in a pan with melted butter, a pinch of salt and a tablespoon of lemon juice, for a few minutes only. Serve immediately with thin slices of buttered brown bread.

DUNDEE

There was an old woman who lived in Dundee,
And in her back garden there grew a plum tree;
The plums they grew rotten before they grew ripe,
And she sold them for three farthings a pint!

Plums are not featured prominently in Dundee fare but there was a woman – not all that old though – who was responsible for creating the recipe for Dundee Marmalade way back in the 1790s. The lady in question was Mrs Janet Keiller, the wife of a Dundee grocer. One day her husband returned home with a bargain buy; he had acquired a cargo of Spanish oranges for a very nominal sum. Alas, the oranges being of the Seville variety, were rather bitter and did not sell well in the Keiller's shop. So rather than waste the fruit, Mrs Keiller, a woman of Scottish thrift, decided to experiment in her kitchen, and duly concocted a recipe for orange marmalade. She had already established a good trade for her quince preserve known as 'marmalet' and the same customers soon flocked to buy her new product. In 1797, Mrs Keiller and her son, James, set up a company to make marmalade. The Scottish company is still thriving today and exports the legendary marmalade all over the world. Marmalade is *the* preserve for breakfast, and is a sticky affair as Paul Jennings records in *Even Oddier*: 'When numbered pieces of toast and marmalade were dropped on various samples of carpet arranged in quality, from coir matting to the finest Kirman rugs, the marmalade-downwards-incidence varied indirectly with the quality of the carpet.'

The following recipe is a good basic one for Seville orange marmalade, should you be unable to buy a jar of Mrs Keiller's.

Marmalade

2lb (900g) Seville oranges
1 lemon, or 2tbsp lemon juice
3½ pints (1.760l) water
3½lb (1.575kg) preserving sugar

Wash the oranges (and lemon if using a fresh one) and cut them into halves, then quarters and finally chop to make shreds as thick or thin as you like. Carefully remove any pips and tie them in a muslin bag. Put all the chopped fruit into a preserving pan, or very large saucepan, with the water, lemon juice if not using fresh lemon, and pip bag. Simmer for 2hr when the peel should be soft and the liquid reduced by about half. Discard the pip bag and add the sugar, stirring until it has completely dissolved. Bring to the boil and boil rapidly until setting point is reached. Leave to cool for 15min. Transfer to jars and cover in the usual way.

Dundee Cake is believed in some way to be a by-product of the marmalade. The originator is unknown; however, it appears that he or she, lacking certain dried fruits and peel for a recipe, decided to substitute orange marmalade rather than have the cake less rich.

Dundee Cake

8oz (225g) plain flour
Good pinch of salt
1tsp cake spice
6oz (168g) butter
6oz (168g) soft brown sugar
Grated rind of 1 orange
3 eggs
3oz (84g) sultanas
3oz (84g) raisins
3oz (84g) currants
3oz (84g) candied peel or 3tbsp orange marmalade
2oz (56g) halved, blanched almonds

Sieve the flour with the salt and spice and leave on one side. Grease and line a 7in round cake tin with greaseproof paper. Cream the butter and sugar together until fluffy, and add the grated orange rind. Beat the eggs and gradually add to the mixture. Fold in the dried fruits and the sieved flour and spice. Spoon into the prepared tin and make a slight dip in the middle with the back of the spoon. Arrange almonds on top in a circular fashion. Bake in an oven preheated to 325°F (170°C; Gas mark 3) for 2–2½hr. Cover with a sheet of greaseproof after one hour to prevent the top from browning too much. Turn out onto a cooling rack. The cake can be eaten the same day or stored until required.

DUNLOP

Cheese

Dunlop is situated in the Scottish county of Ayrshire, and Dunlop Cheese – a traditional mellow Cheddar type of cheese – is usually regarded as Scotland's national cheese. Skimmed milk cheeses have been made in Scotland from time immemorial, but it was not until 1688 that Barbara Gilmour introduced the method of making cheese with whole milk. The young dairywoman, who had fled to Ireland to avoid the Covenanting persecutions, learnt the method there. When she returned to Dunlop, she started to use her newly acquired knowledge, and farmers whose 'Dunlop' cows (the variety now recognised as the Ayrshire breed) were producing more milk than could be sold, soon started to copy Barbara Gilmour's sweet milk cheeses.

As Dunlop Cheeses were made by so many different people, the end results varied considerably and the qualities were quite erratic. So in 1855, after nearly two centuries of hit and miss production, the Ayrshire Agricultural Association enlisted the aid of a Somerset cheesemaker and his wife to re-educate the Dunlop cheesemakers to make uniform cheeses. This explains the similarities between Cheddar and Dunlop Cheeses, although the latter is slightly softer.

As the railways developed, enabling Scottish farmers to send their milk supplies further afield, the making of Dunlop Cheese lost much of its importance. However, quite a lot is still made, and is available throughout Britain.

DUNMOW

Dunmow Flitch

A flitch is quite simply half a pig. In Great Dunmow, Essex, there is a delightful ceremony, dating back to 1104, which is known as the Dunmow Flitch Trial. It sets out to find a married couple who have lived happily together, without a single quarrel, for at least a year and a day. Several couples

take part and they have to come before a mock jury made up
of six local maidens and six local bachelors. The following
oath has to be sworn:

> You doe swear by custom of confession
> That you ne're made Nuptiall Transgression,
> Nor since you were married man and wife,
> By household brawles or contentious strife
> Or otherwise in bed or at boarde,
> Offended each other in Deed or in Word
> Or in a twelve moneths time and a day
> Repented not in thought in any way
> Or since the Church Clerke said Amen
> Wish't yourselves unmarried agen,
> But continue true and in desire,
> As when you joyn'd hands in Holy Quire.

Since 1445, all successful claimants have been rewarded
with a flitch of bacon. The first flitch award, on record, was
given to Richard Wright by the Little Dunmow Priory
where the ceremony used to take place. Through the years
the proceedings have been moved to Great Dunmow, and
at the recent Trials, the flitch was awarded by the Dunmow
Flitch Bacon Company.

This company first started trading in 1909. The pigs are
bred on farms in Essex, Cambridgeshire, Suffolk and Hertfordshire, and the majority of them are cured into bacon.
The remaining meat is used for pork sausages and pork pies.

Within the factory, the pigs have to be slaughtered,
weighed and graded, and cut up into suitable sizes. Next
they are taken to the curing cellars, where they are pumped
with brine and placed in large curing tanks. After several
days they are lifted out and left to dry. Some of the bacon is
sold to customers like this, but much of it is smoked. On
average, about 700 tons of bacon leaves the factory each week
and the Dunmow Flitch Bacon Company's vans are seen
regularly in south-east England. For the traditional English
breakfast of fried bacon and eggs, Dunmow bacon is hard
to beat.

ECCLES

There are several towns in England called Eccles but it is to Eccles in Lancashire we must go to find the famous cakes. These much-loved (and frequently incorrectly copied) pastry and currant affairs were known in the seventeenth century, and possibly before. They were popular fare at the old Eccles Wake which began on the first Sunday in September and lasted a further three days. Other features of the Wake included bull baiting, donkey racing, cock fights and a fiddling match with a piece of silver for a prize. The old Eccles Wake song goes as follows:

When racing and fighting were all at an end,
To an ale-house each went with a sweetheart or friend;
Some went to Shaw's, others Phillip's chose,
But me and my Moll to the Hare and Hound goes.
CHORUS
With music and cakes
For to keep up the wakes
Among wenches and fine country beaux.

But the gaiety was not to last forever and Eccles Cakes, together with the Wakes themselves, were banned by the Puritans in 1650. These reformers claimed that such frivolities resembled paganism, and that the cakes were far too rich. Christmas mince pies were also forbidden, and Oliver Cromwell even passed an Act of Parliament authorising the imprisonment of anyone found guilty of the crime of eating a currant pie. I understand that this strange Act has never been repealed!

With the passing of the Puritan movement, Eccles Cakes and the like became popular again. A romantic story told by Florence White in *Good Things in England* claims that a housekeeper named Mrs Raffald gave her personal recipe for Eccles Cakes to a servant who had served her well for a wedding present. The girl moved to Eccles and apparently, made a good living by selling cakes made from Mrs Raffald's recipe.

The Old Original Eccles Cake Shop was rebuilt in 1835, opposite the parish church, and was described by Arnold Bennett as 'The Most Romantic Shop in the World'. It is now owned by Bradburn's, an old family firm who claim that they are descendants of the original makers of Eccles Cakes.

Eccles Cakes have been enjoyed by kings, queens, presidents and prime ministers, both in Britain and overseas. The shop receives letters from all over the world, many addressed simply to The Eccles Cake Shop, England. But the correct address for those who doubt the efficiency of the modern post office is Parker-Bradburn Ltd, Eccles, Lancashire. Visitors to the town can gorge hot Eccles Cakes, straight from the oven, at Bradburn's Bake Shop.

Eccles Cakes

8oz (225g) puff pastry
2oz (56g) melted butter
6oz (168g) currants
1tsp mixed spice
2tbsp brown sugar
Milk
Granulated sugar

Roll out the pastry quite thinly, and cut as many 4in rounds as possible. Mix the melted butter, currants, spice and sugar and put a generous teaspoon in the middle of each pastry round. Gather up the pastry to enclose the currant mixture, turn over, and flatten a little with a rolling pin. Make 3 slits in the tops and brush with milk. Sprinkle with granulated sugar. Bake on a greased tray at 475°F (240°C; Gas mark 9) for 12–15min. They are especially delicious eaten hot, and if they get to last a few days, it is best to warm them up again.

EDINBURGH

Edinburgh has two notable rocks – the large one which supports the castle, and the small, sweet one which is one of Scotland's most famous confections.

The story of the small, sweet rock starts in the small village of Doune in Perthshire, where a certain Sandy Ferguson once lived. The young lad took no interest in his father's cabinet-making trade, preferring to mess around in the kitchen making sweets. These became popular with his friends and he soon earned the nickname 'Sweetie Sandy'. He left his home in Doune to set himself up in business, tossing a coin to determine whether he should go to Glasgow or Edinburgh. Thus in 1822, he started his business in Bow, a steep, twisting street between the Grassmarket and the Lawnmarket, just under the shadow of Edinburgh Castle. Later, as trade boomed, he moved to larger premises in Melbourne Place.

Through the years, Ferguson's Edinburgh Rock has earned worldwide fame and the factory in Edinburgh still produces the rock according to the original recipe. Mr I. F. B. Stedman, the firm's present managing director and Sandy Ferguson's grandson, says,

> The sweets are made by boiling up sugar, water, perhaps liquid glucose and colouring in an open copper pan

over a forced draught gas stove. The gas is made hotter by a current of air being blown in the cooker by an electrical fan at the same point as the gas enters.

Edinburgh Rock is somehow daintier and less chewy than seaside rock. In a little tartan box you find an assortment of pastel-coloured sticks. The keeping qualities of the rock are incredible – in some cases it has remained edible for fifty years. Edinburgh Rock can be made at home (but you will not get one of those traditional tartan boxes).

Edinburgh Rock

1lb (450g) granulated sugar
1½ gills (210ml) water
½tsp cream of tartar
Flavourings, eg, essences of vanilla, peppermint, orange, strawberry
Colourings, eg, green, yellow, pink, etc

Stir the sugar in the water, in a large pan, over a moderate heat. When it has completely dissolved, turn the heat up, bring to the boil and add the cream of tartar. Boil until hard ball stage is reached (255°F or 124°C on a sugar thermometer) and add your choice of flavouring and colouring. Quickly pour onto an oiled slab or tray – marble is ideal but is rarely found in the modern kitchen. With an oiled knife, lift the corners to the centre but do not work or stir the sticky mess at all. When it is cool enough to handle, dust your hands with icing sugar and 'pull' the rock until it becomes dull. This will take 5min or longer. Then cut pieces to the required length with oiled scissors and leave in a warmish place for 24hr to become soft and powdery. All very messy but great sticky fun.

Edinburgh is sometimes nicknamed 'Auld Reekie' on account of the old factory chimneys that were once responsible for creating quite an unpleasant fog in the beautiful city. There is nothing unpleasant, however, about this recipe for a creamy dessert with a rather unappetising name.

Edinburgh Fog   (Serves 4)

½ pint (280ml) cream
1tbsp icing sugar
Few drops of vanilla essence
3tbsp crushed, sweet biscuits
2tbsp ground or chopped almonds

Whip the cream until stiff, working in the sugar and essence. Fold in the biscuits and almonds and serve immediately.

Although cock-a-leekie is dished up all over Scotland, an anonymous jingle suggests that it was popular in Edinburgh. And Sir Walter Scott, who was born in the city, mentions the soup several times in his writings. The recipe was possibly devised to make use of the cocks used in the cruel sport of cock-fighting. However, now that this ancient pastime is thankfully obsolete, a boiling fowl is generally used.

Cock-a-Leekie (Serves 4)

1 dozen leeks
1 boiling fowl, trussed
Several pints stock or water
Salt and pepper
1tsp mace
2 rashers streaky bacon, chopped
1 dozen prunes

Soak the leeks to draw out the dirt, then scrub and chop them quite small. Put half of them in a large pan with the fowl, salt and pepper, mace, bacon and enough stock to cover. Bring to the boil and simmer for 2hr. Remove the fowl and add the remaining leeks, and the prunes. Simmer for another 30min while you cut the meat from the fowl, chop into bite-sized pieces, and eventually return to the pan. Serve piping hot.

EEL PIE ISLAND

A largish islet in London's River Thames, opposite Twicken-ham Church, is known as Eel Pie Island. It covers about 2 acres and is 530yd long. Years ago, in more leisurely times, it was a favourite haunt of anglers, elegant boating parties, and excursionists, who used to patronise an inn called the Eel Pie House. Needless to say, one of the specialities of this old establishment was Eel Pie, made with Thames eels and boasting considerable gastronomic fame. The old inn was pulled down in 1830, and replaced by the Eel Pie Tavern.

Eel Pie (Serves 4–6)

8oz (225g) puff pastry
2 Thames eels
2 shallots, skinned and chopped
Knob of butter
Little parsley
Small faggot, chopped

1 level tsp dried nutmeg
Salt and pepper
½ teacup sherry
Water
3 hard-boiled eggs, shelled and quartered
Milk
SAUCE
2oz (56g) butter
2oz (56g) flour
Juice of 1 fresh lemon

Rinse the eels, skin and bone, and cut into hunks. Melt the knob of butter and gently fry the shallots for a few minutes. Do not let them brown. Transfer them to a largish pan and add the chopped eel, parsley, chopped faggot, nutmeg, salt, pepper, sherry and enough water to cover the eel. Simmer for 20min then lift out the eel using a perforated spoon and keep it hot. Strain the stock in which it has been stewing. Make a roux with the 2oz (56g) butter and flour, and slowly work in the stock. Bring to the boil and finally add the lemon juice. Arrange the eel and quartered eggs in a pie dish, and pour the sauce over. Leave to cool. Roll the pastry out and cut rim and lid for the pie dish. Stick on, trim and pinch in the usual way. Brush with milk. Bake at 400°F (200°C; Gas mark 6) for 30min, then lower temperature to 350°F (180°C; Gas mark 4) and bake for another 30min.

There was many a conference on the Twickenham isle to debate whether the pie was better eaten hot or cold. However, no decision reigned supreme for long. When the pie was eaten hot, it was deemed the better way, and when cold, the better way yet again!

EGTON

Gooseberry Society

Egton in Yorkshire is a village overlooking the Esk, and is the home of the Egton Bridge Old Gooseberry Society which was founded in 1800. An annual show, held on the first Tuesday in August, maintains the custom of choosing the most magnificent gooseberry grown by a member of the society. The holder of the prize berry to date is 84-year-old Mr Tommy Ventress, who is described as 'Goosegog Champion of the world' by H. Brown in his poem 'The Gooseberry Man' (1975).

Gooseberries or goosegogs have been grown in Yorkshire villages for hundreds of years, and gooseberry pie is mentioned by Oliver Goldsmith in his eighteenth-century novel *The Vicar of Wakefield*: 'That's a good girl. I find you are perfectly qualified for making converts, and so go help your mother to make the gooseberry-pie.' (See more about gooseberries in the Oldbury section). The following recipe is taken from a 1s 6d Yorkshire Women's Institute recipe book of 1948.

Green Gooseberry Sauce

5 pints (2.84l) vinegar
3lb (1.36kg) green gooseberries
1lb (450g) brown sugar
2oz (56g) mustard
½oz (14g) each tumeric, chillies, pepper, and blade mace
1 nutmeg (grated)
8oz (225g) sultanas
4oz (112g) currants
4oz (112g) salt
2 onions

Boil currants, sultanas, gooseberries, onions, mace, chillies in vinegar until quite soft, bruise and strain, add other ingredients and bottle for use; will keep good for years. Better not to use until made a year. (Anon)

ESSEX

Cheese

> A cantle of Essex cheese
> Was well a foot thick
> Full of maggots quick!
> It was huge and great
> And mighty strong meat
> For the devil to eat.
> It was tart and punicate.
> (John Skelton, 1460–1529)

The poet, we may gather, was not a lover of Essex cheese, but surely it cannot have been that dreadful. Anyway, a great deal of it was made in the fifteenth and sixteenth centuries, from ewe's milk as a rule, and consumed in vast quantities by the lower classes and the people below stairs in large country houses. The cheeses are mentioned in *Life at Ingatestone Hall* by F. G. Emmison who records that two or more of them were eaten each week in the winter of 1551. They were apparently much harder than any other county's cheeses – save for Suffolk's which were considered to be the very worst of all – and very strong-tasting. There is no obvious trace of their being made nowadays.

Whilst those employed below stairs were breaking their teeth on Essex cheese, the folk of leisure upstairs were more likely to have been delicately spooning Essex Silliebube. Although various syllabubs were once favoured, this recipe, copied from an old Essex stillroom book, deserves preservation.

Essex Silliebube (Serves 8)

Take a pint [560ml] of white wine, a pint [560ml] of morning's cream, and a quarter of a pound [112g] of sugar, and put them in a bason and beat them well together, till it come to a froth, then pour it into a silliebube pot, and milk a sufficient quantity of milk upon it, and Let it stand in a cole place till night, for the longer it stands, so it grows not sour, the cleaner the drink will be, and the firmer ye curd.

EVERTON

According to legend, the sweet compound known as Everton Toffy was first made in the Lancashire town of the same name by Molly Bushell around 1759. The girl lived in a small cottage, where she cooked up her famous confection. The recipe, so it is thought, was not of her own invention, but was given to her by a distinguished, albeit nameless, medical gentleman from Liverpool. J. A. Picton lamented about the gentleman's secrecy when writing in *A History of Liverpool* in 1873: 'Would that his name have been handed down to posterity! Many men have had noble monuments erected for far less benefits to the human race.' However, Molly proved herself worthy of the secret recipe and soon Everton Toffy earned much fame and many ardent chewers. The recipe is no longer secret and has become a traditional one.

Everton Toffy

1lb (450g) demerara sugar
1 cup water
8oz (225g) unsalted butter
4 level tbsp golden syrup
Few drops of oil of lemon (optional)

Slowly dissolve the sugar in the water, in a heavy based saucepan, over a low heat. Add the butter and syrup and stir. Continue cooking until the mixture reaches 270–280°F (132–138°C), ie, soft crack stage, and remove from heat. Stir in oil of lemon and pour into an oiled, square tin. When nearly cool, mark into slabs.

Everton Mints

Everton Mints are the brand leaders of the sweet manu-facturers Barker and Dobson. Mr & Mrs Dobson started up as retailers in Paradise Street, Liverpool, on returning from their honeymoon in 1834. Later, when they decided to start making sweets themselves, they moved to Franklin Place in Everton – the same district in which Molly Bushell had lived. The casing of Everton Mints is made from sugar, glucose and treacle, boiled to 300°F (150°C). The cooked mixture is then divided into two – one half is coloured black and the other white – cooled to 180°F (138°C) and formed into strips. Twelve black strips and twelve white strips are positioned alternately to form a rectangle. The softer centre, made from sugar, glucose, condensed milk and vegetable fat, is put on top of the strips with are wrapped together to form a mass of mint weighing 75lb (33kg). This is then fed into a miraculous spinning machine which turns the mass into a long rope of evenly striped Everton Mints each 1in in diameter. Very neat!

Without one of these clever machines one cannot possibly hope to compete with Messrs Barker & Dobson, whose traditional mints are easily obtainable in practically any sweetshop.

FAIRLOP

Fairlop Fair

Fairlop Fair was first instigated in the early part of the eighteenth century by Daniel Day, a block and pump maker, who owned quite a lot of land and property in the neighbour-hood of Hainault Forest on the outskirts of London. A generous man, and wealthy after his midsummer rent collection, he thought it fitting to invite his tenants and friends to a feast of beans and bacon, held under the spreading branches of the huge Fairlop Oak in Hainault Forest. The mighty tree, so it was chronicled 'was 8 fathoms round', and 'spread an acre of grounds', and thus provided an ideal sun shade for the feasting revellers. Mr Day's picnic, held annually on the first Friday in July, soon attracted other parties of picnickers, and by 1725, the event had grown into a full-scale fair with refreshment tents and entertainments.

Towards the end of its days, the Oak became very much the worse for wear, and the picnickers who lighted fires in the tree's hollows were blamed for the tree's dilapidated state. The famous landmark finally fell in a gale in 1820, but the revellers frequented the site annually until the 1850s.

The recipe for Fairlop Tarts is believed to have originated in the refreshment tents at the old Fairlop Fair.

Fairlop Tarts   (Makes 10–12)

PASTRY
8oz (225g) flour
4oz (112g) lard or butter
1oz (28g) caster sugar
Cold water to mix
FILLING
2oz (56g) golden syrup
2oz (56g) butter
1 egg
4oz (112g) cake or breadcrumbs
2oz (56g) currants
1oz (28g) sugar
½tsp baking powder

Rub the flour into the butter and caster sugar, to make a breadcrumb-like mixture. Add sufficient cold water to make a stiff paste. Roll out on a floured board and cut 3in rounds with a cutter. Grease some small tart tins and line with the pastry. Fill with baking beans and bake blind at 400°F (200°C; Gas mark 6) for 8min. Meanwhile prepare the filling. Cream the golden syrup and butter together, and beat in the egg. Mix in the crumbs, currants, sugar and baking powder. Divide between the half-baked cases and return to the oven for 15–20min.

FILEY

Fish is important to the inhabitants of Filey in Yorkshire. Their parish church contains a memorial window in honour of fishermen lost at sea, and has a weatherfish on its tower. It is therefore fitting that they should have an original fish dish for dinner or supper on Good Friday.

Filey Good Friday Fish Dish   (Serves 4)

1lb (450g) cod (the very old version calls for woof or ling)
Water
Squirt of lemon juice
2–3 slices of lean ham
3 hard-boiled eggs
Salt and pepper
4oz (112g) shortcrust pastry
Milk

Boil the fish in water with a squirt of lemon juice until tender. Drain off cooking liquor, strain and save. Flake the fish, discarding bones and skin. Cut the ham into strips, shell and slice the eggs. Layer the fish, ham and eggs in a greased pie dish, making 6 layers in all. Season between layers. Pour in some of the reserved fish liquor. Cover with shortcrust pastry. Brush with milk and bake at 400°F (200°C; Gas mark 6) for 25min, until golden and heated through.

FINDON

Findon Haddocks, or Finnan Haddies as they are sometimes called, take their name from a small fishing village in Kincardineshire, about six miles south of Aberdeen to where they are invariably taken for auction in the fish market. Originally, in the eighteenth century, the fish were dried with the smoke of seaweed by local fisherwives and were called 'findrums', but nowadays, they are more likely to be smoked over peat or oakchips. Unlike the smaller smoked haddock from Arbroath which is cured whole, the Findon Haddock is split and flattened out.

Findon Haddocks

Clean the fish and chop off the heads. Skin and cut into bite-sized pieces. Put in a pan with 2 good knobs of butter for each fish. Season with a little freshly ground pepper. Cover with a lid and stew gently until done – about 10min should be adequate but it depends on the size of the fish. The butter used for cooking the fish can be made into a sauce with some milk and a little cornflour, but not everyone bothers with this. They consider the haddocky butter makes the fish moist enough.

FOLKESTONE

Rumbald Fish

Folkestone is a Kentish holiday resort with a picturesque harbour, a seafront lined with Victorian hotels, and many winding streets leading to the old fishermen's quarters. A local fish custom was recorded in the last century. The fishermen used to choose the eight best whiting of the catch from each boat and sell these fish apart from the rest. The money from these was saved for a feast on Christmas Eve, which was called a 'Rumbald', and consequently the chosen fish were known up and down the country as Rumbald Fish.

Folkestone Pudding Pies are so called, I imagine, because people could not decide whether they were puddings or pies. Years ago they were probably sold at the town's fair which was held in June. To confuse matters they are sometimes called Kent Lent Pudding Pies, because they were once popular during Lent.

Folkestone Pudding Pies

1lb (450g) puff pastry
1 pint (560ml) milk
3oz (84g) fine ground rice
3oz (84g) butter
4oz (112g) caster sugar
6 eggs
Pinch of salt
Grated rind of 1 lemon
3oz (84g) currants

Roll out the pastry and line as many old earthenware saucers, or large patty tins, as possible. The saucers or tins may be lightly greased first. Warm three-quarters of the milk and mix the rest with the ground rice. Add this to the warm milk. Stir in the butter and sugar, over a low heat, until they melt. Remove from heat and allow to cool a little. Beat the eggs – if they are large 4 or 5 will be quite sufficient – and add them to the cooled milk with a pinch of salt and the grated lemon

94

rind. Spoon the custard into the pastry lined saucers and sprinkle haphazardly with currants. Bake in an oven preheated to 375°F (190°C; Gas mark 5) for about 25min.

GLOUCESTER

Cheese

The city of Gloucester has much to offer, including a large, indoor market with much local produce on sale. Butter, made on a local farm, is seen in a huge block, and a slab as large or small as you wish can be bought. Cheese is sold on many stalls, the most obvious choice for the visitor being of course Double Gloucester. The double, in fact, refers to its size – a 'Single Gloucester' used to be made – not to its fat content, as with cream. It is a straw-coloured cheese, with a close texture and is mellow or full flavoured. It takes three or four months to mature. Years ago it was garlanded and paraded round the town during the annual May Day celebrations.

The cheese used to be produced in the Vale of Berkeley, but nowadays it is made in many West Country factories. However, the milk used in these modern cheeses is rarely from the Gloucester breed of cows. These are very rare today – as are the Gloucester Old Spot Bacon Pigs – with only seventy animals surviving in twenty-two herds, but fortunately the Gloucester Cattle Society, originally established in 1919 but defunct after 1945, was reformed in 1973 to foster the breed. The Martells of Laurel Farm, Dymock in Gloucestershire, make real Double Gloucester cheese using milk from their small Gloucester herd, and Mrs Monica Martell tells me that they are the only makers of genuine Double Gloucester in the world. They do not, however, sell their cheese commercially at present but are building up their stock with this in mind.

Double Gloucester – even that made with ordinary cow's milk – is a very good supper cheese and accompanies pickled onions particularly well. I also spotted a variety flavoured with chives – a good alternative for those wishing to avoid oniony breath.

Cheese Rolling

Just outside Gloucester, at Cooper's Hill, a delightful custom, which is many centuries old and involves the cheese, still persists. On Whit Monday, many people gather at the top of Cooper's Hill to compete for a large cheese which is rolled down the hill. It is never caught before it reaches the bottom because it travels very fast, about 70mph! Miraculously, the cheese when claimed by the first to scramble downhill, is still intact. This is because a very hard, well-matured cheese is deliberately chosen for the occasion.

It is thought that originally, the custom was a form of sun worship, the cheese representing the sun. But similar ceremonies, once held in neighbouring villages, were simply observed to mark the commencement of the cheesemaking season.

A traditional way of cooking Double Gloucester is to bake it in the oven with ale.

Gloucester Cheese and Ale for Toast

8oz (225g) Double Gloucester cheese
2–3tsp made mustard
½ pint (280ml) strong ale
Slices of toast

Slice the cheese thinly and lay it in an ovenproof serving dish. Spread the mustard between the layers. Pour on enough ale to cover the cheese and put in a hot oven until the cheese melts and mingles enticingly with the ale. Bring to the table immediately, and let people dig into the bubbling dish and spread some of the delicacy on their toast. Any leftover ale can be used to soften the toast, if liked, and additional supplies can be brought in to drink.

GRANTHAM

In days gone by, Grantham in Lincolnshire was a town of great importance. It was here that the Royal Mail coaches would stop for a while and change their horses. A great number of ordinary folk, travelling up and down the apparently never-ending Great North Road, would pull into Grantham to seek refreshment, or even accommodation for the night.

In the early part of the eighteenth century, visitors to the town would invariably purchase a supply of Grantham Whetstones to munch on their tedious journeys. These were the first biscuits to be offered for sale and gained a fair reputation. However, they were soon to be bettered. It was due to the habit, in that era, of keeping the windows of business premises well shuttered that a profitable discovery was made. A local tradesman, a certain William Egglestone, entered his baker's shop one Sunday in 1740, and set about making some small cakes for his own family. In the dim light, he confused one of the ingredients, and instead of remaining the same size, the cakes were twice as large after baking. It appears that he had added some sort of raising agent, with the flour, in error. Nevertheless, his family, friends, and later on the customers in his baker's shop, all found the new cakes quite delectable. And so Egglestone established a flourishing trade in Grantham Gingerbreads, travellers on the Great North Road much preferring them to the some-what solid whetstones. (Hardly, I would have thought, an appetising name for a cake in the first place!)

Egglestone's original recipe is now in the hands of Catlin Brothers who run the eminent Catlin's Cafe in Grantham's High Street. This house was built in 1560 and it is believed that Captain Charles Hamilton, an officer in Cromwell's army, took refuge here as his pike was found hidden in the building. More important, in my opinion, than any old spear are the gingerbreads. They are pale, gingery and hollow – more like a meringue than a gingerbread – but quite delicious. There are various recipes but naturally Catlins retain their original, and their Granthams are well worth sampling if you get the opportunity. However, this recipe makes white gingerbreads, similar to Egglestone's originals.

Grantham Gingerbreads

8oz (225g) self-raising flour (don't chance finding the baking powder with the curtains drawn!)
1 level tsp ginger
3oz (84g) butter
8oz (225g) caster sugar
1 large egg

Sieve the flour and ginger. Mash the butter with a fork, mix in the sugar, and beat in the egg. Stir in the sieved ingredients and knead to make a dry, stiff dough. Break off walnut sized pieces and roll into balls. Let the warmth of your hands smooth over the cracks – do not be tempted to add any liquid or the gingerbreads will rise and fall sadly in the oven, instead of being dome-shaped and hollow. Place on a large, non-stick baking tray, leaving plenty of room between them to allow them to spread. (When baked they are about 3in in diameter.) Bake in an oven at 300°F (150°C; Gas mark 2) for about 45min. Even when they are sufficiently baked they are still very pale. Leave them to cool and harden before removing from the baking tray as they are apt to stick and break at the base if moved while still warm.

GRASMERE

The picturesque village of Grasmere is sited to the north of the lake of the same name in Cumbria. The traditional Grasmere Gingerbread is still made in the village and sold at Sarah Nelson which is at present owned by Mrs Margaret G. Wilson. The quaint shop was a school run by the church from 1660–1854. When the Education Act was introduced making education compulsory, another school was built in the village and the church allowed Sarah Nelson and her husband to live in the little cottage. Sarah started to bake gingerbread in order to make some money and she sold her bakings to travellers who patronised the inn opposite the cottage. When she died in 1904, aged 88, her two nieces continued to bake the gingerbreads until they sold the recipe to Mrs Wilson's aunt and uncle. Now Mrs Wilson owns the original recipe, which is still a secret and kept in the bank. Thus genuine Grasmere Gingerbread can only be obtained from S. Nelson, Church Cottage, Grasmere, Cumbria. However, the following recipe is in the Grasmere style, being more similar to a shortbread than a normal cake-type gingerbread. It is characteristically hard in the middle and crumbly on top.

Grasmere Gingerbread

8oz (225g) plain flour
½ level tsp each of cream of tartar and bicarbonate of soda
Pinch salt
1 rounded tsp ground ginger
4oz (112g) brown sugar
4oz (112g) butter
1 level tbsp golden syrup

Sieve the flour with the cream of tartar, bicarbonate, salt and ginger. Rub in the butter until the mixture resembles breadcrumbs. Mix in the sugar and the golden syrup. The mixture will appear to be too dry and crumbly, but do not be tempted to add any water. Spoon two-thirds of the mixture into a lightly greased tin, about 8in square, and press down firmly with the back of the spoon. Sprinkle the rest of the mixture on top. Bake in an oven preheated to 325°F (170°C; Gas mark 3) for 50min. Remove from oven and mark into fingers.

GREAT YARMOUTH

Fresh herrings plenty, Michell brings,
With fatted crones, and such old things.

(Thomas Tusser, 1580)

Red Herrings

Great Yarmouth is a prosperous holiday resort on the Norfolk coast. It was once an important fishing town but nowadays, the famous herring fleet is fast dwindling. However, some fish are still brought ashore here, and herrings, in their various forms, can be bought in the large market place.

To the north-east of the market, the historical Fishermen's Hospital can be seen, and on the Quay, the homes of the bygone wealthy fishing merchants still remain.

Commencing in September, the herring season is much later here than further north and in Scotland, where the busiest time is May and June. The regional difference led to the custom of 'the wee Scottish lasses' travelling down to Yarmouth, when the Scottish season had finished, in order to help with the gutting in the south. Their deft handiwork, and the amazing speed at which they work, are greatly admired.

The herring is a truly confusing fish for it can be disguised as a rollmop, bismarck, buckling, bloater or kipper. But of all the herring incognitos it is the bloater and kipper which are most associated with Great Yarmouth (and Lowestoft – see this section also). In the last century, the heavily smoked and highly salted red herring was also popular. However these are not seen very frequently these days, although apparently quite a number are exported. An 1837 edition of the celebrated *Penny Magazine* tells us that once landed,

> they are immediately carted or carried away in baskets to the 'rousing house', adjoining the house where they are intended to be hung and smoked. They are then again sprinkled with salt, and are heaped together with wooden shovels, on a floor covered with bricks or flag-stones, in which state they remain five or six days, and they are then washed, spitted, hung up and fired.

The herrings were suspended by the mouth and gills, and great care was taken to ensure that they did not touch each other. Green wood was often used for the fires which 'must be neither too quick nor too slow and at times they must be extinguished'. Oak and beech were, and still are, considered to impart the best flavour, whereas fir trees or timber from old ships, encouraged the herring to taste bitter.

The method of preserving fresh herrings by smoking is claimed to have been introduced by several inspired persons, but Yarmouth has a popular tale that is worth recording. It attributes the first bloater to a Mr Bishop, a herring merchant in 1835. According to the tale, his employees went home early one day, leaving a good catch of herring unattended. Mr Bishop hastily threw some salt over them, split them through the gills and left them hanging in a chimney near his fire. Next morning he ate a couple for breakfast and was astonished to discover that they had acquired a remarkably good flavour. So instead of chastising his lazy workers, he was full of praise for the discovery that their absence had instigated. Thus the bloater industry in Yarmouth was born. Technically a bloater is a whole herring which is lightly smoked and dry salted, as opposed to the heavy smoking and salting of the red herring. The more delicate treatment results in a silvery-white fish which tastes rather good.

Baked Bloaters

Wash the fish and chop the heads and tails off. Split each fish open and carefully remove the backbone. Spread the inside of each bloater with 2oz (56g) of butter and close up again. Place on an oiled, enamel plate, sprinkle with dry mustard powder and a little chopped onion. Cover with another plate and bake in a moderate oven 350°F (180°C; Gas mark 4) for 15–20min, or until soft. Do not overcook them or they become rather dry. Serve straight from the oven with more butter pats.

Potted Bloater Paste

This is a tasty paste for sandwiches, toast, or even to stuff in potatoes baked in their jackets.

First wash out some small pots or jars. Bake a couple of bloaters as described above. When done, allow to cool enough to handle. Pull off the skins and discard along with any stray bones. Mash with a fork and weigh the fish. Soften the same weight of butter and blend with the mashed fish. Press firmly into the pots and pour melted butter over to seal. Store in the refrigerator.

Kippers or Painted Ladies

Kippers are probably the most popular form of herring and the busy housewife even has the 'boil-in-the-bag' variety at her disposal. Kippers are actually herrings which are split, lightly brined and smoke-cured. Kippers are always sold in pairs. In the southern counties they are generally dyed orange too, earning the nickname 'painted ladies', but in the North this is considered distasteful.

Kippers can be fried, grilled, baked or boiled, but a novel method (and very useful in a power strike when one is perhaps limited to a one-ring camping-Gaz stove) is to immerse the fish, devoid of elegance with their tails up, in a jug of very hot water. They will cook themselves in 4–5min, although you will miss the kipper aroma that accompanies the orthodox methods of kipper cooking. When they are cooked they should be dotted with butter before serving.

Sleeping as quiet as death, side by wrinkled side,
toothless, salt and brown, like two old kippers in a box.
(Dylan Thomas, 1914–53, *Under Milk Wood*)

HAMBLEDON

Wine

Drink no longer water, but use a little wine for
the stomach's sake and thine often infirmities.
(Timothy I, 5 : 23)

In AD 280 the Emperor Probus authorised Roman Britain to grow vines and make wines, and from that time until the dissolution of the monasteries by Henry VIII, British wine was swallowed by the gallon within these shores. However, after that period, home-produced wine lost considerable appeal, almost becoming a joke, and it is only in recent years, thanks to dedicated gentlemen like Major-General Sir Guy Salisbury-Jones, GCVO, CMG, CBE, MC, that British wine has at last rightly re-established itself on our tables. Nowadays, alas, the vineyard at Hambledon, in Hampshire, cannot produce enough wine to satisfy demand.

The first vine was planted at Hambledon in 1952 and the following quote is taken from a detailed paper on Wine-Growing in Britain by Sir Guy.

I am often asked what induced me to plant it. I think that it all goes back to 1917. One day, in the cold wet Autumn of that year, the Division to which I belonged attacked alongside the French, and at the end of the day we found ourselves sharing a muddy slit trench with some French soldiers. These splendid 'Poilus', as they were called, seeing that we had no wine ration, took pity on us and shared with us their own, thereby boosting our morale. Never has wine been more welcome, and on that day was consolidated my love, not only for France, but for her wine.

Sir Guy describes his wine as follows:

We only make one wine here – a dry white wine. My French friends strongly advise me against making a red wine in this northern climate. We have a few black grapes which we blend in with the majority which are white. Incidentally, few people realise that two-thirds of the grapes used for Champagne are black. But the juice or must does not ferment in contact with the skins so that the wine is not discoloured. We now have a very friendly link with Pol Roger of Champagne, one of whose best growers comes over to help us. This is particularly helpful since our chalky soil resembles that in Champagne.

Not surprisingly, the wine from Hambledon is very similar to a still, dry Champagne. Incidentally, the Hambledon vineyard is open to the public on Sundays from the last Sunday in July to the first Sunday in October. (Tel: Hambledon 475.)

HARROGATE

Toffee

Harrogate in the old West Riding of Yorkshire was once famous solely for its mineral springs which were discovered in 1571, but of late, Harrogate toffee is rather better known.

In the year 1840, Mr and Mrs John Farrah lived in a plain, white-washed shop which adjoined the famous old Crescent Inn. Mrs Farrah looked after the grocery and sweet trade whilst her husband worked in a modest bakery. The small business soon earned a reputation for the Farrahs' toffee, and gentlemen, ladies and schoolboys alike, were all drawn to the shop to buy the sweetmeat. Frequently, purchasers' carriages completely blocked the narrow Crescent Road. The toffee was even acclaimed by that shrewd cynic, the late Henry Labouchere, when he referred to his boyhood days in September 1903: 'Of those early days I have two vivid recollections. The one is the smell of the Old Sulphur Well and the other is the taste of Harrogate Toffee, and, needless to say, I dreaded the one as much as I loved the other.'

Harrogate Toffee is made from the best ingredients and contains more butter than many other toffees. It is available from confectioners or from John Farrah at 7, Royal Parade, Harrogate.

HEREFORD

Beef

Hereford retains a certain elegance not usually found today quite simply because it has altered so little with age. A fine example of life many years ago is the Livestock Market in Newmarket Street, which is perhaps the busiest municipal market still thriving in England, dealing with just under half a million cattle annually. The main market day is Wednesday but some trading takes place on most other weekdays as well. Worth a special mention are the Hereford white-faced cattle with their characteristic down-curving horns. The best beef is said to be obtained from a three to four year old animal, and carcasses should ideally be hung for two weeks before being jointed. Hereford beef is especially prized as much of the meat is marbled (the lean is streaked with fat) which produces an excellent flavour.

Cider

Hereford was the birthplace of the flamboyant orange seller, Nell Gwynne, and a plaque on a wall pinpoints the exact location. There is also a huge cider factory which welcomes visitors – write to the Public Relations Dept, H. P. Bulmer Ltd, Ryelands Street, Hereford – but unfortunately there is a very long waiting list. A tour of Bulmer's plant is a fascinating and enlightening experience. Bottles march everywhere, sometimes higgledy-piggledy with impatience as they wait their turn to be sterilised, and sometimes in orderly files as they queue to be filled. The enormous black vats with horizontal white stripes hold anything from 10,000 to 1,100,000 gallons of cider, and there are 235 of them. Bulmers make several types of cider – sparkling, still, dry or sweet – the choice is yours.

Cider is an ancient drink dating from pre-Roman times, and in Celtic mythology an apple god was worshipped. The diarist, Samuel Pepys, records that he 'drank a cup of Syder' on 1 May 1661. But it was not until 1887 that the Bulmer cider-making industry began when Mr H. P. Bulmer, the younger son of the Rector of Credenhill near Hereford, first used the apples from the rectory orchard to make cider. Through the years, Bulmers have grown to be the largest cider-making factory in the world, and have been responsible for planting many thousands of acres of orchards with bitter-sweet cider apples.

The following party drink recipe is by courtesy of H. P. Bulmer Ltd.

Fair Maid of Hereford

1 pint (560ml) Bulmer's Woodpecker (medium sweet) cider
Crushed ice
½ pint (280ml) ginger beer
¼ pint (140ml) orange juice
6 sprigs fresh mint

Cover bases of 6 tumblers with crushed ice. Combine cider with ginger beer and orange juice. Stir. Pour equal amounts into tumblers. Add a sprig of mint to each.

In June, the quietest time of year for the cider industry, Hereford celebrates with a spectacular cider festival.

With cider almost on tap in Hereford it is not surprising that the local cooks use it so readily in the kitchen, and of course, the odd slurp does revive poor souls slaving over hot stoves.

Hereford Cider Cake

8oz (225g) plain flour
Pinch salt
½ level tsp nutmeg
½ level tsp ginger
½ level tsp bicarbonate of soda
4oz (112g) butter
4oz (112g) sugar
2 eggs
¼ pint (140ml) cider

Sieve the flour with the salt, nutmeg, ginger, and soda. Cream the butter with the sugar until fluffy, and beat in the eggs. Whisk the cider to make it frothy and add to the creamed mixture. Fold in the sieved ingredients and blend. Turn into a greased oblong tin, about 8in × 6in, and bake at 325°F (170°C; Gas mark 3) for 45–50min. Once quite cold, it is best to store the cake for a day before cutting it.

HONITON

Honiton Fair

Honiton is a small Devon town of which an attractive Georgian main street forms the backbone. A little of the famous Honiton lace is still made locally; it is sometimes called bone lace, because fish bones were once used to hold the lace in position as it was worked. Honiton is also noted for its fair which is held in late July. It dates from the mid-thirteenth century and still displays the traditional stuffed glove to announce safe trading. The fair opens with a Hot Penny Ceremony during which children scramble for hot pennies which are thrown from windows.

Years ago, fairings was a loose name covering a wide range
of fairground edibles including caraway comfits, candied
angelica sticks, macaroons, almond comfits and various
gingerbreads. Now many of these have faded from ·fashion
but Honiton Fairings remain popular. They are sometimes
called brandy snaps, and in London and the southern counties
they were once known as jumbles.

Honiton Fairings (Makes 10–12)

2oz (56g) flour
1 level tsp ground ginger
2oz (56g) butter
2oz (56g) golden syrup
1 rounded tbsp demerara sugar
2 tsp brandy (optional)

Sieve the flour and ginger together. Melt the butter slowly in
a bowl over a pan of boiling water and add the syrup and
sugar. Stir until the sugar dissolves. Remove from heat and
stir in flour and ginger, and brandy if using. Mix to a paste.
Drop teaspoons of the paste onto a greased baking sheet,
allowing 3–4in between each. Put in an oven set at 350°F
(180°C; Gas mark 4) for 10–15min, when they should have
spread to flat, golden, lacy rounds. Remove from oven and
as soon as they are cold enough to handle, wrap each in
turn round a greased wooden handle, to make little tubes.
You have to work quickly as the fairings cool and harden
rapidly. If necessary, they can be resoftened in the oven.
Some people stuff them with whipped cream, but this should
not be done until just before they are to be eaten otherwise
they go soggy. Sometimes they are not curled at all, but left
flat, which does make storage easier.

HUNTINGDON

Huntingdon, the birth place of Cromwell, lends its name to
a very old recipe for Figit Pie. This can also be spelt Fidget
or Fitchett, and I can only imagine that the name came
about because the ingredients tend to sink and shift about
during the cooking. A pie funnel is therefore essential to
stop the crust from caving in.

Huntingdon Figit Pie (Serves 4–6)

1lb (450g) bacon, streaky or collar
8oz (225g) onions
1lb (450g) apples
Salt and pepper
1 tbsp golden syrup

Water
8oz (225g) shortcrust pastry
Little milk

Discard the bacon rind and dice the meat. Skin the onions and cut into rings. Peel the apples and slice. Place alternate layers of bacon, onion and apple in a round pie dish – about 2–3 pint – seasoning each layer well and remembering the pie funnel. Stir the syrup into a cup of hot water and pour over the other ingredients. Roll out the pastry to make a lid for the pie. Brush with a little milk and bake in an oven preheated to 375°F (190°C; Gas mark 5) for 1½–1¾hr. If the pastry shows a tendency to become overbrown, cover with a piece of foil. Traditionally the pie is eaten hot, sprinkled with sugar.

ISLE OF MAN

Kippers

An old custom called the Quaaltagh was once commonly observed on the Isle of Man, on New Year's Day. All over the island, groups of young men used to go from house to house wishing the people happiness and prosperity for the New Year, in song. Many houseowners invited the merry songsters inside their homes, and offered them the best of food and drink available. A part of the song went as follows:

> May they of potatoes and herring have plenty,
> With butter and cheese and each other dainty.

Also, an old Manx saying declared that eaters of herring and mullet on New Year's Day would have a most prosperous New Year. Thus, it is not surprising to discover that herrings, specially cured as kippers, are the most noted food from the isle. John Curtis of Douglas have been curing herrings for many years, and their curing depot was visited by King George VI and Queen Elizabeth in 1945. The fish are landed at Peel, very early in the morning, and transported straight away to the curers to be kippered whilst still plump and fresh. (A correspondent, recalling childhood memories, describes the old horse-drawn herring carts that once used to trundle from Peel with the 'lill silla fellas' piled high.) Once at the Curtis curing house, they are split up the back, gutted by skilful girls and bathed in brine for a short while. Next they are turned into tenting boxes from which they are hung on long sticks, left to drain, and finally smoked over fires of oak chippings. Manx kippers are a pale lemony colour and Mr Curtis guarantees that no dye is used in the curing. He suggests that they should be cooked in a frying pan, with perhaps just a little fat to start them off. However from June to September this extra fat is not necessary as the fish are so fat that they can easily be cooked in their own oil

JERSEY

Milk and Cream

Jersey is the largest of the Channel Isles and boasts a good sunshine record and much French influence. The early inhabitants were mainly retired or settled sailors and fishermen, who, incidentally, donned the pullovers known as jerseys, hence the name. These early islanders soon recognised the quality of the local cattle, and in 1789, legislation was passed forbidding the importation of live cattle. Thus, on the island, the distinguished dairy cow has remained thoroughbred throughout the centuries, and many herds of them have been exported all over the world. Jerseys produce more milk and butterfat per acre than any other type of cow, and the animals in the island give around three million gallons annually. All the cows in Jersey are registered by the Royal Jersey Agricultural and Horticultural Society in a Jersey Herd Book, which was started in 1886, and the most beautiful of the beasts are shown at the Society's shows in May, August and October. There are many awards to be won including a handsome prize for the 'Best Uddered Cow'.

Jersey milk is much richer and creamier than ordinary milk, and is easily distinguished in the bottle, as it is not treated to stop the cream from settling on the top. Jersey cream is thick and 'moreish', and miniature Jersey cow cream jugs are sold everywhere on the island.

Potatoes, Tomatoes and Cabbages

Because of the mild, sunny climate – not noticeable when I was there for a holiday – Jersey also produces very good early potatoes. The most popular variety grown is the Royal Jersey Kidney Fluke which is white skinned, white fleshed and akin to a kidney in shape. These are exported throughout the British Isles and only require a gentle rub before they are thrown in the pot. Tomato growing is also a flourishing business, and the 'toms', as they are called, are large and juicy, and ripen early. Whilst on vegetables and fruit, I have to mention the peculiar Jersey cabbages. These are grown up to seven feet tall, such height being encouraged by pulling off the lower leaves as they form. The cabbage stalks become very sturdy and those of a suitable size are dried and varnished, and sold as walking sticks.

Before the wonders of agricultural chemicals were discovered, Jersey farmers used to scout the tide-washed rocks for seaweed or vraic – this being the local word – not to eat as in some parts of Britain, but to use as a fertiliser for their crops. As this was quite tiring work, they used to take little buns with them to sustain themselves. Hence the naming of these buns, which do not have seaweed in their ingredients.

Jersey Vraic Buns

1½lb (675g) risen bread dough
6oz (168g) mixed dried fruit
1tsp nutmeg
4oz (112g) sugar
4oz (112g) butter
1oz (28g) lard

Work all the ingredients together. Shape the dough into small buns and put on a greased tray, spacing well. Cover and leave to prove in a warmish place for 15min. Bake at 400°F (200°C; Gas mark 6) for 20–30min.

The next recipe, for Jersey Wonders, is probably the most widely known Jersey recipe, and I take the following from the Jersey Island Federation of Women's Institutes publication, *Bouon Appetit*.

Jersey Wonders

12oz (337g) self-raising flour
4oz (112g) plain flour
4oz (112g) sugar
4oz (112g) butter
4 standard eggs

Sieve the two flours together, then put 3½oz (98g) flour into bowl, add sugar, mix well, add butter, mix well, add eggs and remainder of flour. Make a stiff paste; you may have to add more flour if not stiff enough. It must not be too soft. Roll into little balls, roll flat, make cuts and twist outside inside [see note on next page]. Cook in deep pan with 1½lb (675g) lard. Make all Wonders before cooking as you cannot make and cook at the same time.

Note: Shape the dough into balls the size of a walnut and leave for 30min. Then roll into oblong shapes with a rolling-pin. Make 3 cuts in the middle of each piece and taking the two sides of the dough at the same time, pass under again through the cut in the middles. Some people only make two cuts while others do them by the figure eight method, and others as butterflies. According to certain people, the rising tide has much to do with the success of their Wonders. It is to our knowledge that more than one housewife takes good care to make her Wonders when the sea is going down.

KENDAL

Kendal is often called 'The Auld Grey Town' on account of its grey limestone buildings which predominate in this old Westmorland (now Cumbrian) town. What is not so well known is that this town was one of the pioneers of the English wool industry. The old heavy woollen cloth known as 'Kendal Green' was born here and the town's motto *Pannus mihi panis* means 'Wool is my bread'. Visitors to Kendal should not miss the Castle Dairy in Wildman Street, which is a fine example of domestic architecture of the Tudor period with exposed, carved beams. The house is open to the public in the afternoon and becomes a restaurant in the evening.

Among the impressive list of products which Kendal manufactures are Kendal Snuff and the celebrated Kendal Mint Cake. The latter is a sweetmeat, not a teatime cake, and is produced by four different factories – one of which is Daniel Quiggin & Son, a company that started in the Isle of Man in 1840. It was there, so they claim, that the firm became the first to put letters in rock. When Prince Albert visited the Isle of Man in 1847, Mr W. Quiggin's daughter, Elizabeth, presented His Highness with lettered rock with 'Welcome Prince Albert to Mona' running through the centre. Mr W. Quiggin had four sons and one moved to Kendal and started a business there.

It is not certain when the cake originated but the present Mr Quiggin suggests that his father probably started making the rock some eighty years ago. Described as 'the pack full of energy', Kendal Mint Cake is a favourite with mountain explorers, and is made with white or brown sugar.

Kendal Mint Cake

1lb (450g) sugar, white or brown as preferred
¼ pint (140ml) milk
½–1tsp peppermint essence

Dissolve the sugar in the milk in a pan over a low heat. Boil to soft ball stage (240°F; 115°C). Remove from heat, add peppermint essence and beat until smooth. Pour a thin layer, about ¼in, into oiled, shallow tins or trays. Leave to set a bit and mark into slabs. For convenience it can be chopped into small sweets and wrapped in paper twists. However, traditionally it is always made in oblong slabs and one feels delightfully childish chomping through a bar on the bus.

KENT

Kent Sir – everybody knows Kent – apples, cherries, hops and women.

(Jingle in Charles Dickens' *The Pickwick Papers*)

Hops

The orchards of Kent have earned the county quite a reputation but, as a female myself, I decline to comment on the women. Pounds and pounds of fruit are still grown annually, and travel to markets and greengrocers up and down the country. But perhaps the most important crops are the Kentish hops which are renowned for flavouring many of the great British beers. However, hops have not always been utilised so. Originally they were cultivated purely for medicinal preparations until some traveller brought over hopped beer from the Continent, to oppose the traditional ale. In Henry VIII's time, hopped beer was forbidden and it did not become commonplace until the seventeenth century.

Hops actually determine the bitterness of the beer – the more hops, the more bitter the beer – by adding flavour to the brewed malted barley. Hop vines are grown on a network of strings supported by tall poles. At the start of each season, 'stringers' have the arduous task of securing many miles of string in readiness for the new vines to climb on. When they are ripe, around September, the vines are pulled down and the pickers set about pulling off the cones. Nowadays much picking is done by machine, but Kent was once crowded with East Londoners who used to spend their holidays helping the locals gather the hop harvest. Christopher Smart, a Kentish poet, opened his long Miltonic poem, 'The Hop Garden' (1740) with the following lines.

> See! from the great metropolis they rush,
> The industrious vulgar! They like prudent bees
> In Kent's wide garden roam, expert to crop
> The flow'ry hop.

The hop pickers used to perch themselves on baskets or old camp stools and work as deftly as possible since they were paid by the number of bushels picked, not by the hour. An experienced, fleet-fingered hopper could pick up to twenty bushels a day, and invariably was nicknamed a 'scratcher'. The regulars who came year after year, bringing all the family with them, had large wicker baskets with their initials painted boldly on them. These generally held five bushels and painted rings defined each one bushel measure. Every so often during the day, the tally-man came round to empty the baskets and tally up the hops. These were then turned into large green sacks for transportation to the oast house for drying.

Sad to say, it is not quite the same today, and only a handful of people make the annual trip to Kent as mechanisation now presides. However, if you wish to view the modern hop-picking operations' Whitbread's hop farm, Beltring, is open to visitors by appointment, for a period of three weeks in September. The visit includes a tour of the hop garden and oast house which is in Tonbridge; application should be made to Public Relations, Whitbread & Co Ltd, Chiswell Street, London EC1Y 4SD.

Wine

A much newer Kentish speciality is another alcoholic drink, Kentish Sovereign Wine. This is made at Cherry Hill Vineyard which was only established in 1966 in Nettlestead. In 1970, 4,500 bottles of white wine were produced from local grapes grown on vines originally imported from Germany and France, but the output is increasing all the time. Visitors are welcome here too, but strictly by prior appointment. Apply to Kentish Vineyards, Cherry Hill, Nettlestead, Kent.

Now to something non-intoxicating, and ideal for a staunch teetotaller's afternoon tea, Kentish Huffkins. These are oval doughnut shapes made from a light bread mixture and originally came from east Kent.

Kentish Huffkins   (Makes 5-6)

1lb (450g) plain flour
1tsp salt
1½oz (42g) lard
¾oz (21g) fresh yeast
1tsp sugar
½ pint (280ml) warm (not hot) milk and water mixed

Warm a mixing bowl. Sift in the flour and salt. Rub in the lard and make a well. Cream the yeast with the sugar, and a little of the warm liquid. Add the yeast liquid to the flour, etc, with enough warm milk and water to stir to a soft dough. Knead until smooth. Cover with an oiled polythene sheet and leave in a warmish place to double in bulk, about 45-60 min. Grease a baking tray and flour well. Shape the risen dough into oval cakes – this quantity makes 5 or 6 – and make a hole in the middle of each. Place on prepared tray, spacing well, cover and leave to prove again, about 10min. Uncover (I mention this because a friend of mine, in her usual haste, forgot to remove the polythene and the mess in the oven was grim) and bake at 400°F (200°C; Gas mark 6) for 15min. Traditionally huffkins are wrapped in a clean cloth when they are taken from the oven, until they are cool. This ensures their characteristic soft crusts, and makes them ideal for the toothless. Serve them with butter and jam, like any other teacakes.

KINGSTEIGNTON

Ram Roasting Fair

A Ram Roasting Fair is held at Kingsteignton in Devon on Spring Bank Holiday Monday. A whole ram is paraded through the streets to the side of Oakfield Meadow where it is roasted whole, amid the general chaos of a more ordinary fair with stalls and entertainments. The custom is believed to have originated when the local stream, running through the church yard, dried up. The priests advised a sacrifice to induce the stream to gush forth again, which it apparently did.

LAKE DISTRICT

Charr Pyes

Of all the freshwater fish to be caught in the Lake District, the charr is the most unusual and least known. They are colourful fish and are in season from July to October. At present they are not very fashionable and are hard to obtain outside the areas where they are fished, but in the nineteenth century they were used to make a fish soup which was held in high esteem and served at notable banquets. Before then, charr pyes were much favoured and large quantities were regularly sent to London. These were made by steaming the fish, removing all the flesh, and mixing it with melted butter, like a potted fish. It was seasoned with salt and pepper and flavoured with mace or lemon juice and a little cream was sometimes added to make a richer filling. Then it was encased in pastry – or sometimes smoothed into special charr pots which were invariably decorated with a picture of the fish – and baked in the usual way.

LANCASHIRE

In the past Lancashire Hot Pot was made in a tall, straight-sided, earthenware pot, often with the words 'HOT POT' figured in the clay on the outside. It was one of those country dishes that was frequently left on the fire to simmer away happily by itself, until required by the menfolk returning home after a long day working out on the land. However, according to one or two old references, some enterprising farmers used to take a steaming hot pot with them in the morning, and bury it in a haystack to retain its heat for a midday meal in the fields. Oysters were always included in past centuries, when they were cheap fare, but they can be

omitted, and indeed usually are nowadays, without signi-
ficantly spoiling the taste of the stew.

Lancashire Hot-Pot   (Serves 6)

2lb (900g) middle neck of lamb
4 lamb's kidneys
2lb (900g) potatoes
1lb (450g) onions
10–20 oysters (optional)
Salt and pepper
1 level tsp curry powder
1 level tsp sugar
½ pint (280ml) stock
Dripping

Chop the meat into cutlets, trimming off surplus fat if not
liked. Skin kidneys and slice. Peel and halve 3 or 4 potatoes
to top the hot pot, slice the rest 'as thin as a penny'. Skin
and slice the onions. Warm an oven-to-table casserole in
the oven. A Hot Pot is always served at the table from the
pot in which it has been cooked. Melt a large knob of dripping
in it and slosh it around to coat the inside of the pot. Layer
the cutlets, kidneys, potatoes, onions, and oyster if using,
seasoning well and sprinkling with curry powder and sugar.
Top with the halved potatoes. Pour in the stock and brush
the top potatoes with a little melted dripping. Cover with
lid or foil and cook at 350°F (180°C; Gas mark 4) for 2¼–2½hr,
removing the lid for the last ½hr to get the potatoes 'right
browned off by the fire'. Traditionally the dish is always
accompanied by a large jar of pickled red cabbage to offset
any fattiness.

A Lancashire Foot was originally devised for miners to
eat in the pits. A substantial hunk of grub for hard working
men, it takes its name from the shape of the pastry before it
envelops the filling. The Lancashire writer, Joan Poulson,
quotes an amusing snippet from a magazine of 1900 in her
work, *Old Lancashire Recipes*. 'She's left his Foots in t'oven
and they're burnt to cinders'. This seems to establish that
two foots were foots and not feet. Anyway, a pair of foots
was usually made at a time from a large oval of pastry which
was cut in half lengthwise, with the longer side running
north to south. The rolling pin was then positioned at the
equator, on each of the two pieces in turn, and the cook
rolled northwards to make the wider toe part of the foot –
the south remaining unrolled and thicker, to resemble the
heel, and to make a firm base for the filling. The toe piece
was then folded back over the heel, and being wider, easily

encased the filling. The elliptical pasties were carried down the pits in little oval tins. Many different fillings were used and two of the most popular are given below.

A Pair of Lancashire Foots

1lb (450g) shortcrust pastry, rolled out as described above
FILLING I
4tbsp chopped onion
4oz (112g) cubed Lancashire cheese
4oz (112g) chopped bacon or leftovers
Salt and pepper
Dry mustard
Milk

Combine the onion, cheese and bacon and season to taste. Sprinkle with a little mustard. Divide between the 2 heels. Brush round the outer edge of the toes with milk. Wrap the toe parts over, tucking under, and pinch to seal. Brush with milk and bake at 375°F (190°C; Gas mark 5) until brown and inviting.

FILLING 2
8oz (225g) lean beef, or leftovers, chopped
3 medium potatoes, peeled and cubed
2tbsp chopped onion
Salt and pepper
Little stock
Milk

Mix the meat, potatoes and onions and season well. Simmer in a little stock until meat is cooked. Allow to cool and then continue as for the first filling.

Lancashire Cheese is often claimed to be the best cooking cheese in the world. It does not separate like some, and therefore is especially suitable for toasting – resulting in the nickname Lancashire Toaster – for sauces, and for sprinkling on soups and stews. Some cooks like to strew some broken pieces over their hot pots. The best Lancashire Cheese, so it was often claimed, was made at Leigh in Lancashire, and was fittingly known as Leigh Toaster, but little or no cheese is made in Leigh nowadays. In fact, only about 150 Lancashire Cheeses are made per week, and two separate days' curds are used in the process. In times of depression, the cheese was a major source of protein for the working classes. When there was no meat for the hot pot, a vegetable soup was made and cheese was crumbled on the top just before serving. Its clean, mild flavour makes it a fine cheese to complement sherry and wines, and also to mingle with herbs.

Lancashire Potted Herb Cheese

8oz (225g) Lancashire Cheese
2oz (56g) butter
4tbsp thin cream
Good few slurps of sweet sherry
Fresh herbs such as chives, thyme, sage, etc

Chop the herbs. Crumble the cheese into a metal basin. Add all the other ingredients and stand the bowl over a pan of simmering water. Stir until creamy then pour into little pots. Cover when cold. This is very good spread generously on biscuits, wafers or toast.

Pace Eggs

An unusual old custom is still observed in Lancashire at Easter. Known as pace-egging, it involves the rolling of hard-boiled eggs downhill, and one venue is the Aveham in Preston. The eggs are decorated and the idea is to get your egg to roll as far as possible without cracking. Owners of cracked eggs have to forfeit them to owners of sound eggs, who promptly eat them!

LEICESTER

Red Cheese

It is the deep orange-red colour of Leicester Red Cheese that makes it so attractive. Displayed with other paler cheeses, it is apt to appear like a sun-bronzed body, just returned from the Bahamas in the middle of an English winter, making all the other poor souls appear anaemic. The milk that is used for making Stilton Cheese is also suitable for making Leicester Red. In fact, Leicester Red Cheese may have developed as a method of using up milk not required by the Stilton makers. Traditionally, a Leicester Red was shaped like a grindstone, being about 20in in diameter and 6in deep, and weighing about 45lb, but nowadays the cheeses are invariably smaller. The cheese ripens quite quickly, only taking from ten to twelve weeks to reach a stage when it can be eaten, and is fully matured in six months. It has a mild flavour and is especially good for making Welsh Rarebit.

Another speciality, prominent in Leicester and neighbouring Midland towns, is the variety of cheesecake which just does not seem to exist further south. The cheesecakes are not made with cheese at all, but are a cross between a puff pastry tart and a lemony flavoured fruit cake.

Leicester Cheesecakes   (Makes about 12)

8oz (225g) puff pastry
1 egg
1½oz (42g) butter
1½oz (42g) sugar
Grated rind of 1 lemon
1oz (28g) cake crumbs
1½oz (42g) ground almonds
1oz (28g) currants
½tsp cinnamon
2tsp pure lemon juice
2tsp milk
Few drops of almond essence

Grease some small cake tins. Roll out the pastry, cut 3in rounds, and use to line the tins. This recipe makes about a dozen cakes. Separate the egg and put on one side. Cream the butter and sugar together until light and fluffy. Beat in the egg yolk, lemon rind, crumbs, ground almonds, currants and cinnamon. Add the lemon juice, milk and almond essence, and mix well. Fork the egg white until it holds its shape and fold into the mixture. Put a walnut-sized blob in each pastry case. Do not be tempted to be more generous as the mix rises considerably and too much only makes very messy looking cakes. Bake in an oven preheated to 375°F (190°C; Gas mark 5) for 25–30min.

LEIGH-ON-SEA

Cockles

The old quarter of Leigh-on-Sea in Essex, is a real old cockle town with fishing boats at rest and suitable sea orientated pubs like the Smack and the Peterboat. On fine summer evenings the narrow main street swarms with locals and visitors alike, all intent on a plate of cockles and a pint of beer. The cockles are dredged from the sands facing Leigh, the Southend and Shoebury mud flats, and the eastern shores of Canvey Island.

The cockles, with their shells tightly shut, are steamed until they open and then are shaken in a wire sieve until the poached bodies drop through to a cleansing brine. In 1978 fifteen pence would buy a small plate of cockles from one of the counters at the front of the old cockle sheds. There is no local recipe. People just eat them with their fingers, some sprinkling them with salt, pepper and vinegar. On the beach behind the sheds are piles of cockle shells, profitable by-products which are sold for road-surfacing and the like.

Crafty local folk use the shells more artistically to make shell animals and figurines in crinolines, which are sold as souvenirs. Some even plant the shells in their gardens.

> Mary, Mary, quite contrary,
> How does your garden grow?
> With silver bells and cockle shells,
> And pretty maids all in a row.
>
> (Trad. nursery rhyme)

LINCOLNSHIRE

In many towns in Lincolnshire years ago, Plough Monday (the first Monday after the twelfth day of Christmas) was celebrated gaily. Local folk used to dress up as 'plough wags' in carnival-style costumes, and go around in groups knocking on people's front doors whilst reciting various ditties. This was the local rhyme spoken by the Hobby Horse:

> In comes I who's never been before,
> If you give me your best beer, I'll never come any more.
> And I am hungry as well as dry
> And should like a bit of your best pork pie.

Hand-raised pork pies are still popular in Lincolnshire and the following recipe by Mrs M. C. Fulford of Lincolnshire is taken from the *Rescue A Recipe* booklet by courtesy of the Women's Royal Voluntary Service.

Lincolnshire Pork Pie

3½lb (1.575kg) plain flour
1½lb (675g) lard
Pinch of salt
¾ pint (420ml) water

Rub ½lb (225g) lard into sifted flour, add a pinch of salt. Boil together 1lb (450g) lard and ¾ pint (420ml) water. Place flour in a warm mixing bowl, make a hole in centre and pour on boiling liquid. Knead well and leave to cool slightly, then shape into pies on jam jars or moulds.

FILLING
4lb (1.800kg) fat and lean pork
1oz (28g) salt
¾oz (21g) pepper
½ pint (280ml) water
Stock from trimmings and pork bones

Pass meat through coarse mincer then season with pepper and salt and add water. Fill pie cases, cover with pastry and decorate edges and top, making a hole in the centre. Brush over with egg. When cool pour in jelly (made from trimmings and bones) through top of the pie lid. Oven temperature: 300°F (150°C; Gas mark 2) for 2hr till gravy boils.

Pigs used to be kept by many people in this county – and not so very long ago at that. It was customary to kill off the fattened animals in late autumn or just prior to Christmas, and a slaughter was an important date in people's diaries. Much of the pork was salted down for the winter months, and the rest of the animal – in fact *all* of the rest of the animal except the squeal – was utilised in some way or another. Even the bladder was blown up and used as a football! The perishable bits and pieces surplus to the family's needs were given away to neighbours as 'Pig's Cheer'. The neck of the pig, sometimes called the chine, was stuffed, and this dish is still quite common in Lincolnshire. A chine has to be taken from the carcass before the animal is split, so alas can only be obtained from a butcher who does his own butchering.

Stuffed Chine

1 neck chine of bacon
Quantity of fresh parsley
Little thyme and majoram
Few spring onions

Soak the chine in cold water for 24hr. Dry and score both sides. Put the other ingredients, washed and picked, through a mincer and stuff them into the scores. Wrap the joint in a cloth, tie securely, and boil for 3½–4hr, depending on size. Slice and eat when cold. Some recipes suggest covering the stuffed joint with a flour and water paste and baking it in the oven. The crust is then discarded. However, this method seems a bit wasteful in this time of food shortages. A stuffed chine was once the traditional county dish at the old, almost forgotten, local feasts, one of which was always held on Trinity Sunday. One of these communal repasts was authentically revived at Osbournby in 1969, in order to raise money for church and chapel, and participants plan to relive this old tradition annually. The same dish was formerly favoured by many families during 'May Day', the local name for the first week in May.

LIVERPOOL

In thirteenth-century Lancashire, Liverpool attracted certain attention as a small fishing village, but now the place has grown to become a huge seaport with seven miles of docks. Liverpudlians are often dubbed as scousers and one of the city's best known recipes is for Scouse.

Liverpool Scouse   (Serves 6)

1oz (28g) dripping
1½lb (675g) stewing beef, cubed
1lb (450g) onions, skinned and quartered
8oz (225g) carrots, scrubbed and chopped
1 turnip chopped
1½lb (675g) potatoes, peeled and quartered
Salt and pepper
Stock or water to cover

Put the dripping in a large pan and melt over a high heat. Toss in the meat and brown quickly, and evenly, by turning the cubes around. Add the prepared vegetables and plenty of seasoning, and cook for another minute or so. Add enough stock to cover, bring to the boil, cover and simmer for 2–3hr. It is best to let it cool so that the fat can be scraped off the top, and to reheat it thoroughly before serving. In Liverpool pickled red cabbage is often served with scouse – the vinegary sharpness matches the scouse's richness rather well.

Peg's Leg is course slang for a wooden leg, but it is also the name for hard twists of Liverpool Toffee which were common fare on market stalls twenty-five years or more ago. This toffee is striped and flavoured with peppermint.

Liverpool Peg's Leg

8oz (225g) dark brown sugar
8oz (225g) golden syrup
8oz (225g) black treacle
6oz (168g) lard
2tbsp malt vinegar
1 level tsp ground ginger
½tsp baking soda
Few drops of peppermint oil

Into a large, heavy based pan, over a very low heat, put the sugar, syrup, treacle, lard and vinegar. Do not stir, but leave it to its own devices until all the ingredients have dissolved to a good gungy mixture. Bring to the boil, and let it bubble away with the occasional stir, until it reaches a hard set. Pour half the toffee into another warm pan and stir in the ginger rapidly. Pour onto a well oiled slab or tray. Add the baking soda and peppermint oil to the remaining toffee in the pan. Stir until it rises white and then pour this on top of the dark toffee. Working very quickly, pull it out, working lengths of light and dark toffee into striped twists. Cut off short or long pieces as you like best. Leave to cool and harden.

LONDON

Two old Bachelors living in one house;
One caught a Muffin, the other caught a Mouse.
(Edward Lear, 1812–88 in *Nonsense Songs*)

In Victorian and Edwardian London, the Muffin Man was one of the most patronised street vendors. He would announce his arrival – in a manner similar to, but more tuneful than, today's ice-cream vans – by means of a large brass handbell, and my uncle remembers how, as a child, he used to anticipate hopefully the ringing around 4 o'clock to liven up Sunday afternoons, in the 1920s. The muffins were carried on a large tray, skilfully balanced on flat hats worn by the Muffin Men.

London Muffins (Makes 12)

1lb (450g) plain white flour
Good tsp salt
½ level tbsp sugar
Bare ⅓ pint (187ml) tepid milk, plus extra if necessary
2tsp dried yeast
1 egg, beaten
2tbsp butter, melted

Sift flour and salt together. Dissolve sugar in ⅓ pint (187ml) tepid milk and shake in the yeast. Fork a little and leave to froth, about 10min. Make a well in the flour and salt and stir in the yeast liquid, egg and melted butter. Mix into a softish dough, adding more milk if necessary, and knead well on a floured board for 10min or until the dough loses its stickiness. Cover and leave in a warmish place, or in the refrigerator overnight, to double itself. Knuckle out any air bubbles and roll out about ½in thick. Cut into 3½in rounds. Cover and leave to prove again. Heat up an oiled griddle or thick frying-pan, and cook on each side for 6–7min. Split with the fingers and serve warm, oozing with butter, or beef dripping.

Incidentally, Dickens speaks of the 'United Metropolitan Improved Hot Muffin and Crumpet and Punctual Delivery Company' in Chapter 2 of *Nicholas Nickleby*, and muffins

and crumpets are often muddled with each other. However, generally speaking, a muffin is much the thicker and requires splitting, whereas a crumpet is quite thin and does not. Muffins are made from a dough, and crumpets from a batter. Both were found in the old nursery tearoom, and were toasted on long brass forks in front of burning orange coals. Latterly, the word 'crumpet' has become a word used by the male sex to describe a fancied female. If George Bernard Shaw is to be believed, the muffin has a much staider reputation. He wrote in *Man and Superman*: 'Marry Ann; and at the end of the week you'll find no more inspiration in her than in a plate of muffins.'

London Crumpets

1lb (450g) plain flour
1tsp salt
1 pint (560ml) plus 2tbsp milk
½ level tbsp sugar
2tsp dried yeast

Sieve flour and salt together. Warm milk to blood heat – no more – remove from heat and stir in sugar to dissolve. Sprinkle with yeast and leave until frothy. Make a well in centre of flour and salt, and pour in yeast liquid and mix well. Cover the batter and leave in a warmish place for 45min. Grease a griddle, and crumpet rings if you like to use them. Spoon tablespoons of the batter onto hot griddle and cook until brown on underside and bubbles appear on top. Do not flip over. Serve toasted with butter. They store well, untoasted, in the freezer, and for a change they can be turned into mini cheese and tomato pizzas without much ado.

London Buns are, these days, plain long finger buns with

white or pink icing, but through the years the name has been used to describe several yeast buns – albeit not the distinguished Chelsea Bun – containing various dried fruits and peels. Theodora Fitzgibbon in *A Taste of London* gives an old recipe for interesting spicy, orange-flavoured buns called London Buns. There is also the old tale about 'Mr London Buns' related by the late Florence White in *Good Things in England*. Briefly, she explains how an odd piece of bread dough was shaped to represent a little man with currants for eyes, buttons, etc, and one day this doughy chap – also called a Johnny Cake – escaped from the kitchen whilst the cook was away, by executing a brilliant series of cartwheels. Mr London Buns and the legend are now forgotten, but this recipe for London Buns can be used to make Mr London Buns if you fancy reviving a tradition.

'The variety and names of buns are determined by the skill and ingenuity of the bakers.' (J. Kirkland in *The Baker's ABC* (London 1927)).

London Buns

1lb (450g) strong plain white flour
1tsp salt
1½tsp dried yeast
1tsp sugar
¼ pint (140ml) milk
¼ pint (140ml) water
1½oz (42g) melted butter or margarine
Water icing

Sift the flour and salt. Warm the milk and water until tepid, move off heat and stir in sugar to dissolve. Sprinkle on yeast and leave until frothy. Pour into the bowl of flour and salt, along with the melted butter. Mix to a pliable dough and turn on to a floured board. Knead with floury hands until no longer sticky. Cover with an oiled polythene sheet and leave until doubled in size. Knead the risen dough and shape into finger buns, about 4in long. Put on a greased baking sheet, well spaced, and leave to prove again. Bake at 425°F (220°C; Gas mark 7) for 10–12min. When cool, coat with sticky water icing.

Chestnuts

London may have lost her Muffin Men but street-sellers of hot chestnuts are still prominent, especially in the winter around Charing Cross Road and Regent Street. The chestnuts are traditionally roasted in the old-fashioned way on charcoal stoves, throwing out a welcoming warmth for Christmas shoppers with icy hands.

Jellied Eels

Also sold from street stalls, frequently near pubs, is the cockney favourite, jellied eels. There is an old saying that babies in East London are weaned on them! It is apparently a lucrative trade; Sheila Hutchins records the Jellied Eel King, Robert Cooke, who had an eel and pie stall in Horseferry Road before World War II died leaving £42,000, quite a fortune in those days. Tubby Isaac's stalls are popular nowadays and I even found one exiled in Clacton, Essex.

Eels can be jellied at home but no one seems to do it. Far better to buy from those who spend their lives preparing those huge white enamel bowls of the delicacy, and to eat them out of doors in the street where they taste better anyway. Eel pie and mash (see Eel Pie Island section) can still be had from the slowly diminishing number of Eel and Pie Shops, not forgetting the 'liquor' – a greeny mixture flavoured with parsley and much loved by the East-enders.

Oysters

On St James' Day large quantities of oysters are eaten by Londoners, but their children are content to use the shells for building grottos and to illuminate these by means of rush lights. The children ask passers-by for contributions to the grottos. This is an annual custom, but it lasts several weeks, to the annoyance of pedestrians.

(from *Times Telescope*, 1823)

Oysters too, are very much Londoners' fare, at least they were in Johnson's day when they were so cheap that the famous doctor was able to feed his cat on them for two old pennies a day. Now of course, they are very expensive, but if you care to blue whatever modest fortune you have on them on St James' Day (25 July), an old saying promises that you will not want for money during the year.

Steak and Kidney Pudding

Oysters were always included in the rather special Steak and Kidney Pudding that was once made annually by Dr Johnson's favourite pub, Ye Olde Cheshire Cheese in Wine Office Court, off Fleet Street in London. The pudding, so the establishment claims, was first made in 1775, and then again for many years until the 1930s. This magnificent pudding weighed in at between 50 and 80lb and also boasted grouse, mushrooms and many other ingredients to help the steak, kidney and oysters down the hatch. Traditionally the first pudding of the year was made in October to coincide with the onset of the cold British winter, and through the years many distinguished persons have been invited to make the first cut with considerable ceremony. In 1975, the gastronomic ritual was revived by the *Daily Mail* newspaper, with Vincent Mulchrone doing the honours. I quote from the *Daily Mail* dated 18 October 1975, a few of Mr Mulchrone's words:

> The knife was sharp. I weigh 15 stone. Yet my first thrust barely penetrated its four-inch suety crust. When I dug deeper there rose an aroma with the majesty of an olfactory symphony.
>
> If you think of the general run of steak and kidney puds as an 'A' on a single violin, this was like breaking into the 1812 Overture when the artillery comes in.

Gin

In past centuries the problem of continual gin-guzzling was widespread – the cockney slang for gin is 'mother's ruin' – but of course many laws, regulations and taxes throughout the years have taken care of the problem. London has its own special dry gin distilled by James Burrough.

The name gin is derived from genever or genièvre which are, respectively, the Dutch and French translations of juniper; the juice of juniper berries is one of the basic ingredients of gin. A seventeenth-century Dutch physician, Dr Franciscus Sylvius, must be credited with the production of the first authentic gin, which he made for medicinal purposes and called Aqua Vitae. The doctor's medicine was soon sampled by British soldiers fighting in the Low Countries: they declared it to be a good substitute for English beer which they were unable to obtain, and even took some back to England. Thus the gin-drinking habit was established when William of Orange became King of England in 1689, although the sale of gin was still mainly through chemists, who recommended it as a cure for kidney complaints, gout and rheumatic disorders, to name but a few.

Then in the early part of the nineteenth century a pharmaceutical chemist, James Burrough, founded the House of Burrough distillery in Chelsea. He chose the Beefeater for a brand name because he wanted something synonymous with tradition and prestige as well as typical of London.

Throughout the nineteenth century, London Dry Gin gradually overtook the already popular Dutch gin, which eventually lost favour. When James Burrough died the family partnership was formed into a limited liability company, and to this day is still very much a family concern.

LOWESTOFT

Bloaters, Kippers and Herrings

Like Great Yarmouth in Norfolk, Lowestoft in Suffolk is noted for its herring industry, and the various forms of cured herrings. For the method of dealing with bloaters and kippers, see the Great Yarmouth section, as although in different counties, the two towns are within ten miles of each other and recipes are similar. In Lowestoft two smoke houses still operate, one in Raglan Street and another in St Peter's Street, and street names like Herring Fishery Score help to maintain the nostalgic atmosphere of the herring heyday.

The fishermen were quite naturally fond of eating herrings and used to tuck into buckets full of freshly fried fish with gusto. A cook at sea would waste no time in gutting, topping and tailing the fish and finally slitting along each side with a jack knife, then throwing them in the hot frying pan. The sizzling fish were eaten by the ravenous crew with their fingers rather than cutlery, as if the latter was used no hand would be ready to steady the plate if the sea was rough. It was quite usual for a fisherman to get through a dozen fish at one sitting and one much-famed Lowestoft fisherman, Amos Beamish, nicknamed the Giant of Barnby, once ate 100 fish for a bet.

Herrings can be cooked in numerous ways but are very good if simply boiled in salted water for 10–15min. Mustard Sauce is the traditional accompaniment in Lowestoft.

Mustard Sauce for Herrings

1oz (28g) butter
1 level tbsp flour
1 rounded tsp dry mustard
Pinch of salt
½ pint (280ml) fish stock or water
2 tbsp wine vinegar

Make a roux with the butter and flour, in a pan over a low heat. Remove from heat and work in the mustard and salt. Add the stock and wine vinegar and mix well. Return to heat and gradually bring to the boil, stirring continuously. Pour over boiled herring just prior to serving.

LYTH VALLEY

South of Lake Windermere in the Lake District lies a fertile area known as the Lyth Valley. Here grow some of the very best damsons in Britain – known locally as Witherslack damsons, they are large and juicy, and much sweeter than normal damsons. They are used locally in numerous recipes, many of which appear in *Lakeland Cookery* by Jean Seymour, including one for Damson Chutney, which is used here with the author's kind permission. It is an unusual chutney and it goes well with Lancashire Cheese.

Damson Chutney

3lb (1.360kg) damsons
2 pints (1,120ml) malt vinegar
1½lb (680g) peeled and cored Bramley apples
1lb (450g) onions
2tsp ground ginger
3tsp salt
1lb (450g) sugar
1oz (28g) pickling spice

Simmer damsons in half the vinegar until tender enough to remove the stones. Add finely chopped apples and onions, ginger, pickling spice (tied in muslin) and salt. Continue cooking until everything is soft, add sugar, and then the rest of the vinegar. Boil steadily until thick. Put into hot jars and seal down.
NB Jars that have previously held manufactured pickle and chutney are by far the best. Yield: 6–7lb (3–3.5kg). Keep three months before using.

MALDON

Salt

Maldon in Essex is situated right on top of the River Black-water, which is probably one of the saltiest rivers in Britain due to the extensive mud flats in the area. The mud flats are first covered by the tide, and then, as the waters recede, are exposed to the sun and sea breezes which cause rapid evaporation to produce very saline water. The pattern continues as the tide returns to mix with the salty water harboured in the shallow pools. To help the process along, the area has a lower than average rainfall, and the sea water is barely diluted.

Salt harvesting in Maldon and at other places along the Blackwater was probably carried out 2,000 years ago, and the Domesday Book chronicles many salt pans in the area. The early salt makers simply collected the saline water in shallow salt pans, left them exposed to the elements, and let natural evaporation take place. But gradually more care has been taken, and nowadays, the perfect salt crystals are produced under hygienic conditions.

The Maldon Crystal Salt Company was established in 1882 by Mr T. Elsey Bland, who chose to concentrate on producing a specialised crystal salt rather than compete with the large rock salt industries in Cheshire. Mr Bland had his new style salt analysed by Dr Hassell, and subsequently, there appeared in *The Lancet* dated 5 January 1884 the following glowing report.

The Maldon Crystal Salt Company. The salt obtained from Maldon in Essex is sold in white and well defined crystals. It appears to be almost pure chloride of sodium. The traces of sulphate and of magnesium salts in it are so minute that it is non-deliquescent and free from bitter after-taste commonly noticed in the salt used for culinary purposes. We have no hesitation in recommending it for household use, for it is pure as well as attractive.

After several changes in ownership, the business is now controlled by Mr C. B. Osborne, who joined the concern as a workman in 1933, aided by his son, Mr C. C. Osborne, as Managing Director. The company's storage pools are filled at each fortnightly spring tide, when the water is at its deepest and strongest, and then after careful filtering, the water is drawn into large, shallow, steel pans. The salt crystals eventually form after the controlled heating and purifying operations have been affected, and are sought after by discerning gastronomes all over the world.

The following recipes are by courtesy of the Maldon Crystal Salt Company Ltd.

Salt-Baked Chicken

To bake a chicken in salt, cover the base of a large ovenproof casserole with Maldon Sea Salt to about 1in (2.5cm) deep. Place the chicken (which should have been trussed and stuffed if liked) on top and then completely cover the chicken with more Maldon Salt. Cover the casserole with a lid and place on the middle shelf of a moderately hot oven, 375°F (190°C; Gas mark 5) for a 5–6lb (2.2–2.7kg) chicken, bake for 2–2½hr. At the end of the cooking time the chicken will be golden-brown and dry on the outside and the flesh moist and succulent.

Sea-Salt Butter

6oz (168g) unsalted butter
1 rounded tsp Maldon Salt
1tbsp chopped parsley
1tbsp chopped chives

Blend all the ingredients together and chill until firm. Serve with baked potatoes, fried or baked fish or on plain omelettes.

MALVERN

Malvern Water

Water from the Malvern Hills is just about the purest natural water to be found in Britain. Its purity is due to the hard, pre-Cambrian rocks which make up the Malvern Hills. Being so hard, no small particles contaminate the water, which flows freely from many springs. This was first discovered in 1757 by Dr John Wall. There is an eighteenth-century rhyme that reads:

> 'Malvern Water', says Dr. John Wall,
> 'Is famed for containing just nothing at all.'

The water from the Malvern Wells is said to have certain curative powers. In the mid-nineteenth century, a water cure known as hydrotherapy (which originated in Austria) was brought to Malvern by two doctors. One of them, Dr Wilson, established a water cure practice in Belle Vue Terrace, where a bank now stands.

Several wells can be seen today, including Holy Well and St Ann's Well. The latter is said to have been discovered in 1086, but its accompanying cottage (which is now a café) was constructed in 1813.

Schweppes have been bottling and selling (exclusively) Malvern Water for over fifty years. They have a factory adjacent to the Colwall Springs, at the bottom of the Hills, and at one time they used to bottle the water from St Ann's Well. However, if you take the beautiful walk up to St Ann's Well, you can drink the pure water from a fountain for free! (A condition of the surrender of the lease in 1960 stated the new landlords should not be able to sell the water.)

MANCHESTER

A friend's Mancunian brother is a staunch supporter of Manchester City, whose colours are blue and white; he firmly refuses to eat bacon or other 'red and white' meat, because red and white are the team colours of Manchester United, his football team's closest rivals!

There are several versions of Manchester Pudding – maybe tactful housewives have to choose the colour of the jam with care. The following version, however, does not have a pastry base.

Manchester Pudding   (Serves 4 – 6)

1oz (28g) butter
1 pint (560ml) milk
½oz (14g) sugar
3oz (84g) fresh white breadcrumbs
Grated rind of 1 lemon
2 egg yolks
4–5tbsp any jam
2tbsp sweet sherry
2 egg whites, whisked stiff
1oz (28g) caster sugar

Melt the butter in a saucepan and add the milk and ½oz (14g) sugar. Stir to dissolve. Add the breadcrumbs and lemon rind and bring to the boil. Remove from heat. Use a fork to mix the egg yolks with a little of the boiled milk mixture in a small bowl. Pour into the saucepan and return to a low heat. Stir continuously until the custard thickens. Warm the jam and sherry in another pan. Lightly butter a flame-proof serving dish – about 2 pint capacity – and pour half the warmed jam into the base. Next pour on the custard, and lastly the remaining jam. Re-whisk the egg whites until they are stiff and fold in the caster sugar. Dot tablespoons of the meringue on top of the jam in blobs. Bake in an oven at 325°F (170°C; Gas mark 3) for 15–20min, when it should be set. Bring to the table either hot or cold.

Manchester Cob

Another Manchester speciality is quite recent, dating back only to 1973. During the Manchester Festival, the Master bakers of Manchester organised a competition to find a new loaf to be called the Manchester Cob. The winners of the contest were Bill and Sam Ward, who run a bakery in Blackley, and are also famous for their election muffins (see Blackley section). The Wards now sell about 800 Manchester Cobs each week, and other Manchester bakers also bake this award-winning loaf.

MANSFIELD

Mansfield, now one of the prime industrial areas in the North, was once a small settlement in Sherwood Forest. There is a romantic tale that Henry II became lost in the Forest while out hunting. By chance, he met a miller who, not recognising His Majesty, gave him a venison pasty which he joked was made with the King's deer. The King, so the legend claims, was much amused by the miller's unknowing *faux pas*, and he later knighted the 'honest' man.

Mansfield Pudding is one of those 'great British Puddings from the North' that were once indispensable dinner-time afters, but have waned of late. However, local interest was revived in Mansfield a few years ago when a Scottish girl, who moved to the town and attended the Secondary Modern School at Ravensdale, re-discovered the pudding in a history book.

Mansfield Pudding   (Serves 4 – 6)

2oz (56g) fresh breadcrumbs
3oz (84g) plain flour
3oz (84g) shredded suet
1tsp nutmeg
1oz (28g) caster sugar
4oz (112g) currants
2 eggs
½ pint (280ml) milk
1tbsp brandy or sherry

Mix all the dry ingredients together in a bowl. Beat the eggs and stir into the milk with the brandy. Pour the liquid into a well in the dry ingredients and mix thoroughly. Butter a deepish pie dish and fill with the mixture. Bake for 1hr in an oven preheated to 350°F (180°C; Gas mark 4). Turn out and serve with custard or cream.

MARKET HARBOROUGH

Market Harborough in Leicestershire has many fine old buildings including the old grammar school, an unusual gabled affair, supported on wooden pillars under which, in days gone by, a local butter market flourished. A recipe associated with the town is not often found in print, but as a newspaper appeal ascertained, it is still made locally. I even received a letter from a schoolboy who assured me that he often had Pork and Apple Pie for his dinner.

Market Harborough Pork and Apple Pie
(Serves 4)

1lb (450g) pork
Oil for frying
2 large onions, sliced
1 teacup chopped celery
Salt and pepper
½ pint (280ml) stock
1tbsp Worcestershire sauce
2 large cooking apples
8oz (225g) shortcrust pastry
1tbsp flour
Milk

Cut the pork into cubes or bite-sized pieces, and brown in the oil in a frying pan. Add the sliced onion, chopped celery and a little more oil if necessary. Season well. Cook over a high heat for a minute or so. Reduce heat and add stock and Worcestershire sauce. Cover and simmer for 30min. While this is cooking, peel, core and slice the apples, and put half in the bottom of a pie dish. Roll out the pastry to make a lid to fit the dish, and cut 1 or 2 fancy shapes from any trimmings. Leave on one side. When sufficiently cooked, transfer the pork, onion and celery to the pie dish and top with the remaining apple slices. Add 1tbsp of flour to the juices in the frying pan and stir to make a thickish gravy. Pour over the ingredients in the pie dish. Cover with the pastry lid, sticking the edges down with water. Brush with milk. Bake in an oven preheated to 400°F (200°C; Gas mark 6) for ½hr.

MARLDON

Apple Pie Fair

The Marldon Apple Pie Fair was first held in 1888. It was revived in 1958 following a lapse of a number of years. Originally, this Devon fair was a community party, organised to make use of the many windfall apples that used to be available when Marldon was surrounded by orchards. The apples were sliced and cooked together under one huge pie crust. The pie was then cut into hundreds of pieces and sold to cottagers for 'a penny a plateful'. Nowadays, instead of one large pie, many individual pies are baked, and these are stored under a make-believe pie crust. The 'pretend' pie is then carried on a donkey cart to the fair where a celebrity is usually invited to cut the 'crust'. In 1973, the little pies sold for 4p plain or 6p with a dollop of cream – Devonshire of course – and 2,000 were sold in no time at all. The fair is held on or near to 24 August.

MELTON MOWBRAY

Medeltone and Meltone sounds a rather fanciful name for a town, but in fact, Melton Mowbray was once called this. The unusual name most probably originated from two lords who once resided in the town. Although the town's name has become condensed to fit into modern style, the town itself retains much of its olde worlde charm. Many knowing visitors make a beeline for Nottingham Street where 'Ye Olde Pork Pie Shoppe' is prominently situated. At present owned by Mr Young, the site has been used as a bakehouse of some description since the 1600s. I was lucky enough to be allowed behind scenes to watch an employee, Mr Cursley, 'raise' some pies with enviable skill. This is done in the old fashioned way with the aid of a squat, toadstool-shaped wooden block. The traditional Melton Mowbray Pork Pie is made without a tin, or metal band, but simply stands on a baking tray, in the oven, where miraculously it does not collapse. A very slight rounding of the sides is permitted so that the pie takes on its famous 'bellied' shape.

It could be true to say that the invention of the Melton Mowbray Pork Pie may be due to the making of Stilton Cheese, which occurred first in Melton and on surrounding farms before gaining fame at Stilton's Bell Inn. An outlet for whey, a by-product of the cheese, had to be found and eventually it was fed to the pigs who thrived on it. Thus pig breeding increased dramatically in popularity, and an industrious pork market was established. Pork pies became a local speciality and Melton Mowbray has been associated with the fare ever since.

According to legend, the first commercial Melton Mowbray Pork Pie was made by one of two old ladies who lived opposite a baker's shop where they found a suitable commercial outlet. However, neither one of the old ladies would acknowledge that the other had made the first pie, and eventually the contrary pair refused to talk to each other.

Melton Mowbray Pork Pie   (Serves 4–6)

1 or 2 pig's trotters
4 fluid oz (112ml) water
4oz (112g) lard
10oz (280g) plain flour
Pinch salt
1lb (450g) pork, mostly lean
1tsp essence of anchovy
Salt and pepper
2tsp dried mixed herbs
Small egg for glaze

Put the pig's trotter(s) in a saucepan and cover with water. Bring to the boil and simmer for a couple of hours to make a good jelly when it cools. This can be done the day before you make the pie if convenient. In another pan heat the measured amount of water and lard, stirring until the lard has melted completely. Immediately the liquid boils tip in the flour and salt and beat vigorously. Turn onto a floured board, once it has turned to a dough, and when cool enough to handle, knead for about 5min. Break off a quarter of the pastry and put on one side in a covered bowl. Shape the rest into a ball. Now comes the tricky bit which Mr Cursley performed so expertly. First make a drip in the top of the ball with your thumbs, and gradually ease in a large greased and floured jam jar or similar pot with about a 4in diameter – assuming of course that you do not possess one of these little toadstool blocks. Work the pastry about 3in up the sides of the jar until it is reminiscent of a squat beaker without a handle. Carefully remove the jar and put your precious mould in the refrigerator to set for at least ½hr. If, however, by sheer misfortune the wretched stuff will not 'raise' for you without subsiding in an unresponsive way, the only alternative is to enlist the aid of a small cake tin – about 5in in diameter – and line it with the uncooperative pastry. But this is really cheating. Chop the pork into cubes. Do not mince it or the whole thing will taste wrong. Season with salt and pepper, sprinkle with herbs and stir in the anchovy essence. Preheat oven to 425°F (220°C; Gas mark 7) in plenty of time. It is essential that the high temperature is reached before the pie is put in. Roll out the remaining pastry for the lid and cut a 'rose' or 'leaves' from the scraps. Remove the pastry shell from the refrigerator. Pack with pork closely inside. Dampen the top edges, and position the lid, pinching the edges together to seal. Make a small hole in the top of the pie and cover with the pastry 'rose'. Beat the egg and brush over the pastry to encourage a tan. Place in oven. After 40min reduce the oven temperature to 375°F (190°C; Gas mark 5) and cook for approximately 1½hr longer. Remove the pie from the oven and carefully dislodge the 'rose' to reveal the hole. Using a funnel, pour in as much of the jellied stock as possible, just warmed so that it will pour, but definitely not hot. Replace the 'rose' using a little beaten egg or milk if necessary. Leave the pie to cool completely before cutting into slices as required.

MONMOUTH

Although several recipe books describe a Monmouth Pudding the inhabitants have never heard of it. We can only guess that the recipe has died with its originators. The museum at Monmouth has a poster describing a local pudding made for children at the Coronation celebrations of Queen Victoria. This, however, was a curranty affair, unlike any of the Monmouth Pudding recipes I have come across. But even with such an uncertain history, this recipe is too good to be omitted.

Monmouth Pudding   (Serves 4–6)

8oz (225g) freshly made, white breadcrumbs
¼ pint (140ml) milk
2oz (56g) butter
2oz (56g) sugar
Few drops of vanilla essence
2 egg whites
½ jar strawberry jam

Grease a round oven dish, a soufflé dish if you have one, and set oven at 300°F (150°C; Gas mark 1–2). Bring the milk to the boil and pour carefully over the breadcrumbs. Leave to soak for 5min. Meanwhile, slowly melt the butter in a pan and beat the egg whites until they are stiff. Fork through the saturated breadcrumbs to break up any lumps, and add the melted butter, sugar and vanilla essence. Fold in the egg whites. Fill the soufflé dish with alternate layers of jam and breadcrumb mixture, making 4 or 6 layers as you wish, but finishing with the breadcrumb mixture. Bake in preheated oven for about 25min until the top layer is set. Serve immediately as the concoction is similar to a soufflé in texture, and is liable to sag if left standing around.

MORECAMBE BAY

'I shall be but a shrimp of an author', wrote Thomas Gray in a letter to Walpole on 25 February 1768. Today a 'shrimp' is a name for a tiny person. Bought fresh and colourless, straight from the sea, shrimps should be boiled in salted water for 5min until they turn a pretty pink. Then of course the odd bits have to be discarded, which takes quite a long time; one invariably finds very few picked shrimps left at the end because one has eaten so many during the laborious procedure. Morecambe Bay, off the north-west coast of England, is renowned for its shrimps which are potted, and sent all over the world, by several local firms.

Potted Shrimps

6oz (168g) butter
1 pint (560ml) picked shrimps
Good pinch each of salt, nutmeg, mace and cayenne pepper
Clarified butter

Slowly melt the butter over a low heat and toss in the shrimps. Shuffle them around until they are all glossy but do not cook them. Add the seasonings and stir. Transfer to little pots – old yoghurt cartons will do if you have nothing more elegant to hand, though do let the shrimps cool down a bit or they may melt the plastic – and top with clarified butter. Leave to set and serve with brown bread and butter and crispy lettuce. The yoghurt pots are good for picnics.

Flukes

Less famous than the shrimps are the flat fish known as flukes which are also brought ashore at Morecambe Bay. Some people liken them to plaice and they are indeed very good if they are simply cleaned and fried in butter. However, they do not give up easily, and I quote Jean Seymour from her *Lakeland Cookery*: 'Be warned, they die slowly; the first ones I was given lay on a plate and gasped at me the whole of one afternoon until in desperation I went out. Now I can thump them on the head like any other Cumbrian'.

NEWCASTLE

Salmon

Newcastle Salmon is a bit of a misnomer as it does not really originate from Newcastle at all, but from the River Tweed which flows into the North Sea many miles north of the town, at the Scottish/English border (see Tweedmouth section). In the past, the fresh salmon were transported south from the Tweed to the Shields by pack horses, and were simmered there in the famous pickle liquor before being sent on to London and other destinations. It was claimed that the characteristic pickle would preserve the fish for up to a year. The salmon cutlets were stewed in water and strong beer, to which bay salt and common salt were added, then left to marinade overnight. Next day they were put into pots and the pickle made up with strong alegar, pepper, nutmeg and cloves.

Pease pudding is very much a part of Newcastle. Although often described as the national dish of the North-East, and eaten all over Northumberland and Durham, huge bowls of pease pudding are always associated with Newcastle butchers. The locals eat generous servings with sausages and bacon, but most of all with pork. The latter combination has spread south, to some extent, and Johnson enjoyed the dish. 'Pork and peas pudding', he enthused, 'is a conjunction of viands which does not owe its popularity either to old habit or to the mere taste of the epicure'. In less bespoke language we have:

> Pease pudding hot,
> Pease pudding cold,
> Pease pudding in the pot
> Nine days old.
> Some like it hot,
> Some like it cold,
> Some like it in the pot
> Nine days old.

As a child I recall being compelled to eat a ghastly mush called pease pudding at school dinners. I imagine that the stuff must have come out of a tin – and *was* nine days old – because I rather enjoy the following recipe from a Newcastle inhabitant.

Newcastle Pease Pudding   (Serves 4–6)

1 pint (560ml) split peas
2oz (56g) butter
Salt and pepper
1 large egg

Soak the peas overnight in water. Tie loosely in a pudding cloth and boil in more water for 2hr. Drain well. Push through a sieve, beat in the butter and egg, and season to taste. Tie up rather more tightly in a floured cloth and boil for 1hr. Alternatively, smooth into an oven dish and bake alongside the joint for 45min.

NORFOLK

Whether slender or portly, the people of Norfolk are commonly nicknamed 'dumplings', possibly because of the Norfolk race's love for dumplings.

Alas, the very poor ate dumplings alone, minus any meat. Basically, Norfolk Dumplings are made from knobs of risen bread dough which are dropped in boiling water for about 20min. In the past it was common practice to eat dumplings and gravy before the main course – like the eating of Yorkshire Pudding before the main course in Yorkshire. Children were cunningly promised more meat if they ate more dumpling first.

Norfolk Dumplings

6oz (168g) self-raising flour
2oz (56g) breadcrumbs
4oz (225g) shredded suet
1tsp salt
Water to mix

Mix all the ingredients to make a softish dough which leaves the sides of the bowl clean. Break off small balls and drop into the bubbling stew, or alternatively, a pan of boiling water. Cover and cook for 15–20min. The dumplings are apt to join up in the water as they swell, but they should never be cut with a knife; this makes them compressed and heavy. Instead, tear them ruthlessly apart with two forks.

This is a typical present-day Norfolk recipe. The old style dumplings were always made with risen bread dough, but few housewives have time for this these days. Some modern recipes also include an egg, but traditionalists frown on this while accepting the raising agent in self-raising flour.

Turkeys

> Turkeys, carps, hops and beer
> Come into England all in one year.

The most noted Norfolk fare these days is the plump Norfolk turkeys which are always in great demand for Christmas dinners. The bird's association with Christmas started in England in the early seventeenth century, but there are records of its having been served in the early sixteenth century when it was known as the Ind-cock or Indian Peacock. The turkey comes from Central America and its name came about as, in early days, it was frequently confused with the guinea fowl of Turkey. The birds have, since their importation, been most successfully raised in both Norfolk and neighbouring Suffolk, although the former county's name always predominates for some reason. Before the railways were developed, large flocks of the birds were driven from the two counties to the London markets. The drovers kept the creatures heading in the right direction by the use of long sticks with red material 'flags' – turkeys will avoid red objects at all costs.

For the table, the carcass is stuffed from each end, invariably with parsley and thyme stuffing at one end, and sausagemeat at the other. It is a good idea to cover the top of the bird with strips of fatty bacon as the meat has a tendency to dryness.

NORTH RIDING

The old-fashioned pepper cake is still made in the moorland districts of the North Riding, in the East Riding it is unknown. It is a kind of gingerbread, more pungent than the Yule cakes of other districts, but has nothing to do with pepper, at least not at the present time. When the pepper cake is eaten at Christmas, in the moorlands of North Riding, cheese is always put beside it on the table.
(Marmaduke C. F. Morris in *Yorkshire Folk Talk*,
2nd edition, 1911)
This old quotation helps to explain the jingle:

> A little bit of pepper cake,
> A little bit of cheese,
> A cup of cold water and
> A penny if you please.

The following recipe is taken from the Yorkshire Women's Institute's cookery book.

Pepper Cake

1½lb (675g) flour
8oz (225g) moist brown sugar
1tsp Pearl Ash, melted in a little milk†
1oz (28g) powdered cloves
1½lb (675g) treacle
8oz (225g) butter
5 well beaten eggs
† pearl ash is an old-fashioned bicarbonate of soda
Mix all the ingredients together with the well beaten eggs
and bake in a mould or tin in a moderate oven 350°F
(180°C; Gas mark 4) for 2hr.

NORTHUMBERLAND

Haggis

Until lately, it was a common custom in Northumberland
and other parts of the north country to have haggis at
breakfast on Christmas morning, it is now served at
dinner on that day. Haggis was sold at Newcastle
market. The haggis is sometimes made of fruit, suet
and minced liver, heart and other internal parts, or
sometimes oatmeal, suet and sugar, stuffed in a sheep's
stomach and boiled.
(John Trotter Brockett in *A Glossary of North Country
Words*, 1825, Newcastle)

The above quotation does rather squash the common misunderstanding that haggis is Scottish through and through,
although of late it appears to have emigrated to Scotland. As
far as can be ascertained, no haggis is made in Northumberland nowadays. However, the pan haggerty – most probably
deriving its name from the same root as haggis (see Scotland
section), as it too consists of hacked up bits and pieces – is
still a favourite local dish.

Northumberland Pan Haggerty   (Serves 4–6)

1lb (450g) potatoes
8oz (225g) onions
1oz (28g) dripping
4oz (112g) grated cheese
Salt and pepper

Peel and slice the potatoes, and skin and slice the onions.
Melt lard in a frying pan and swirl it round to coat the pan.
Place the sliced potatoes on the pan's base, then the sliced
onions, and top with grated cheese. Season each layer well

as you go. Cover pan with a lid and fry gently for 30min. Remove lid and brown under a grill for 10min. Traditionally this is served straight from the pan.

Another Northumberland recipe with a striking name is Singin' Hinnie. In the past this was baked on an oiled griddle but a heavy-based frying pan can be used instead. The name hinny or hinnie is a north country corruption of honey, as a term of endearment, and the singin' is blamed on the cake's musical humming as it cooks itself.

Northumberland Singin' Hinnie

8oz (225g) self-raising flour
Good pinch of salt
2oz (56g) lard
2oz (56g) butter
3oz (84g) currants
Milk to mix

First grease a heavy-based frying pan and put on a low heat to warm through. Sieve the flour and salt together and rub in the fats. Stir in the currants. (Some recipes also include 2oz (56g) sugar. This is not traditional but can be added at this stage if a sweet scone is preferred.) Add sufficient milk to make a firm dough. Squash into a round cake about ¼in thick and put in the hot pan. Cook gently until the underside is brown. then flip over and brown the other side. Serve piping hot in great hunks, split and dripping with butter.

Hule-doos, Hogmanays and Stotty Cakes

An old Northumberland custom of giving children Hule-doos (or Yull doos or Hyul-doos) was once observed at Christmas, or Yuletide. These were little men or dolls, sometimes symbolising the baby Jesus, made out of ginger-bread or dough. Children also received special festive cakes on the last day of the year. These were known as Hogmanays and were still popular in the late nineteenth century. Yet another treat originally for the children, was a Stotty Cake. These were made to satisfy hungry young mouths that could not wait for the bread to rise and be baked. Housewives used to roll out a bit of partially risen dough, not too thinly, put it on a greased tray and bake at 425°F (220°C; Gas mark 7) until brown and hollow sounding when tapped. Stotty Cakes are still made and sold in some bakers' shops in Northumber-land, and parts of Durham too. They are often eaten with fried bacon at breakfast, or spread with butter, syrup or jam for tea.

NORWICH

Mustard

The use of mustard is very ancient in origin (see also Tewkesbury section) and there are a number of recorded references to it many centuries BC. For example, there is the amusing story of Darius, who in 336 BC gave Alexander the Great a bag of sesame seed to symbolise the number of his army. Alexander was quick to answer with a bag of mustard seed; not only to indicate the number in his army, but also the hot, fiery energy of his soldiers!

In 1742 a mustard factory was established by Messrs Keen at Garlick Hill (I smell a contender here) in London. The Keens were automatically associated with mustard for the entire century and it is probably correct to assume that the phrase 'as keen as mustard' originated from them.

In competition with the Keens, Jeremiah Colman first started to mill mustard at Stoke Holy Cross, four miles south of Norwich, in 1814. A move was made to Carrow in 1854, where the first of many large mustard mills was established, and in 1903, J. & J. Colman took over Keens' business. This mill operated until the early 1950s when the present site in Norwich was commissioned.

Two strains of mustard which Colman's have cultivated are known as Stoke and Kirby, after the two Norfolk villages in which the breeding work was carried out.

Colman's English Mustard is very 'hot', unlike the French of German style mustards, which have vinegar, herbs and spices added to the mustard powder. It is a traditional condiment for ham and beef but goes well with other meats – if you are keen enough to try it!

NOTTINGHAM

Nottingham Goose Fair

Nottingham is set in the heart of Robin Hood country, and Sherwood Forest and Nottingham Castle are much visited sights. Famous also are the beautiful Nottingham lace and the Goose Fair. The latter originated in the thirteenth century and was so called because of the large numbers of geese that were periodically sold there prior to Michaelmas.

> Whoso eats goose on Michaelmas Day
> Shall never lack money his debts to pay.

Before the calendar was advanced by eleven days in 1752, Michaelmas Day was 10 October, whereas nowadays it is 29 September. But the Goose Fair is still held on the first Thursday in October and lasts for three days.

Less famous are two pubs in Nottingham – The Trip to Jerusalem, which is reputed to be the oldest pub in England, and The George, which still has the cheque with which Charles Dickens paid his bill – and the local recipe for Apple Batter Pudding which has recently been revived.

Nottingham Apple Batter Pudding   (Serves 4)

2 large eggs, separated
3 rounded tbsp flour
Pinch salt
½ pint (280ml) milk
4 small cooking apples
1oz (28g) sugar
1 level tsp nutmeg
1 level tsp cinnamon
1oz (28g) butter

Make a batter by mixing the egg yolks with the flour, salt and milk. Leave on one side. Grease a deepish pie dish – the apples should not poke up above the sides. Peel the apples and scoop out the cores, but do not cut them up at all. Lay them in the prepared dish. Mix the sugar with the nutmeg and cinnamon, and cream with the butter. Use this to stuff the apples. Whisk the egg whites until stiff and fold into the batter. Pour quickly, but carefully, over the apples and bake in an oven preheated to 400°F (200°C; Gas mark 6) for 45–50min. Serve sprinkled with sugar and, when occasion warrants it, have a jug of cream whipped with 1tbsp of port on the table.

OLDBURY

Years ago many more gooseberries than nowadays were found growing wild. These berries were very small, weighing no more than ¼oz, whereas modern cultivated ones weigh 1oz or more. In the sixteenth century, the wild berries were used to make a broth, probably some sort of fruit frumenty. The fruit were also valued for their curative powers and Gerard in his *Herball* writes that they were 'greatly profitable for persons troubled with hot, burning ague'.

Oldbury Gooseberry Tarts come from Oldbury-on-Severn in Gloucestershire, and were once very popular at the old Whitsuntide fairs which flourished in the vicinity. They were filled with the wild gooseberries which ripened around Whitsun, and were unusual in that they were made with hot water pastry, which is used quite commonly for raised meat pies but rarely for sweet fruit ones.

Oldbury Gooseberry Tarts

1lb (450g) plain flour
Pinch salt
6 fluid oz (168ml) boiling water
6oz (168g) lard
Small gooseberries – if available, otherwise top and tail some
cultivated ones
Demerara sugar, to taste
Milk

Sieve the flour and salt. Put the boiling water in a large pan over the heat and melt lard in it. Remove from heat, add flour and salt rapidly, and beat very hard. When you have a stiffish dough, turn onto a floured board, and as soon as it is cool enough to handle, roll it out not too thinly. Using a saucer and teacup as guides, cut an equal number of large and small circles. Pleat up an inch on the larger rounds to make self-supporting cases. Fill with gooseberries, and add sufficient sugar to taste, according to sharpness of fruit. Top with the small rounds, pinching the edges to seal. I have found that they are less likely to collapse during baking if they are left overnight in the refrigerator. Brush with milk prior to baking at 400°F (200°C; Gas mark 6) for about 15min, or until golden.

OLNEY

Pancake Race

The Buckinghamshire town of Olney boasts an amusing custom solely for the town's ladies. Any female, clad in a skirt and apron and over sixteen years of age is eligible to run in the famous Olney Pancake Race. The event takes place on Shrove Tuesday – the day when all of Britain eats pancakes. This habit originates from the time when housewives had to use up all their eggs and milk before the Lenten fast commenced. The race is believed to have started sometime in the fifteenth century when a busy housewife, hearing the church bell ring, was so anxious not to be late for the service that she rushed out of her house with her frying pan still in her hand, complete with a sizzling pancake. The local church bell is now nicknamed the Pancake Bell and is rung at the start of the race.

The competitors all line up in the Market Square and have to race down the long, long Church Lane to be greeted by the vicar at the church porch. During the race, the pancake has to be tossed accurately three times, and this understandably does cause quite a batter chaos. Traditionally, the winner receives a prayer book but in 1974, the silver jubilee of the revival of the race by Canon Collins twenty-five years ago, a newly opened bank also presented a cheque for £50.

Pancakes (Makes 6–8)

4oz (112g) flour
Pinch of salt
1 large egg, lightly beaten
2tsp cooking oil (optional)
½pint (280ml) milk
Oil or fat for frying

Mix all the ingredients together in a bowl to make a smooth batter. The oil is not essential but it does make the pancakes easier to toss if you feel so inclined. Oil a pan and put on a medium heat. Turn up the heat until the oil becomes very hot, but not smoking, and pour off any excess. Using a small jug, quickly pour in enough batter to thinly coat the pan. Cook for a minute, or until lightly browned underneath, and then toss over to cook the topside. Serve immediately piping hot. The traditional lemon juice and sugar topping is hard to beat, and for extra zest remember to add the lemon rind, grated, to the juice.

ORMSKIRK

Gingerbread curls take their name from Ormskirk in Lancashire, but were once popular all over the county. In some households, years ago, they were cooked in a tin over an open fire and curled with the poker of all things! They closely resemble brandy snaps, and the fairings from the western counties (see Honiton section), but they are much darker as dark treacle and brown sugar are used instead of golden syrup and white sugar.

Ormskirk Gingerbread Curls

6oz (168g) flour
1 good tsp each of mace and cinnamon
2tsp ground ginger
6oz (168g) butter
8oz (225g) dark treacle
8oz (225g) dark brown sugar
Grated rind of 1 lemon

Sift the flour and spices together. Melt the butter in a pan and stir in the treacle, sugar and lemon rind. Cook until the sugar dissolves completely. Remove from heat and beat in the sifted ingredients, mixing well. Drop tablespoons of the goo onto a greased baking tray, leaving lots of room for it to spread. Bake at 350°F (180°C; Gas mark 4) for 10–15min, or until the edges are crisp and the centres bubbling. Roll quickly into curls with an oiled wooden handle.

OXFORD

Boar's Head

Although the university city of Oxford is moving with the times, the hushed, scholastic image is still very apparent. Maybe it is the numerous colleges. One of them, the Queen's College, is noted for the Boar's Head ceremony at Christmas. A boar's head, or more recently a pig's head, is traditionally prepared, decorated with greenery, and triumphantly served on a large silver platter. A Boar's Head carol is voiced by the college choir and the soloist is presented with the fruit from the boar's mouth.

For a city so large, it is surprising that there are not more Oxford recipes – the scholars must be too busy to eat! However, there are Oxford Sausages which can be made at home, and are far superior to supermarket bangers. These are especially simple to make, providing a mincer can be begged or borrowed, as they are skinless.

Oxford Sausages

8oz (225g) veal
8oz (225g) pork
5oz (140g) brown bread
7oz (196g) shredded suet
Grated rind of 1 lemon
1 level tsp sage
1 level tsp nutmeg
1 level tsp salt
Large pinch pepper
Pinch each of thyme and majoram

Chop the veal and pork, discarding the gristly bits that are a nuisance to chew. Put the meat through the mincer, twice if you like finer textured sausages. Follow up with the bread. This also helps to clean the inside of the mincer and ensures that no particles of meat get left behind. Mix the meat and bread with all the other ingredients and press into a ball. When you are ready to fry, take handfuls of the mixture and roll into fat sausages on a floured board. Fry them in oil or fat until cooked through, and brown and crusty. They make a good meal dished up with fried eggs and beans.

PAIGNTON

Paignton Pudding

A pudding known as the Paignton Pudding or White Pot was once made for the fair at Paignton in Devon. It was a really gigantic affair and the ingredients had to be boiled together in a brewer's copper, rather than in individual bags or skins. What is more, it took up to three days to cook! In 1859, when Paignton's first railway was opened, an extraordinarily huge pudding was made in honour of the occasion. It weighed 1½ tons and consisted of nearly 600lb flour, 200lb bread, and 300lb raisins, as well as large quantities of other ingredients. It took a waggon drawn by eight horses to carry the grand pudding to Paignton Green where the carving ceremony took place. Alas, the vast crowds that gathered became impatient to receive their slices, and surged uncontrolledly forward. A riot followed with lumps of pudding flying chaotically in the melée until every spoonful, or rather fistful, was eaten or beyond consuming.

PLYMOUTH

Gin

One of Plymouth's most admirable assets is the Plymouth Gin Distillery situated in the ancient Barbican area of the Devonshire city. Ever since Queen Victoria's reign, Plymouth Gin has been the Royal Navy's traditional drink. In order to get a true pink gin, many sailors add a dash of angostura bitters.

The distillery's history is fascinating and dates back to 1425, when three monastic orders were established in Plymouth. One of the orders – Black Friars – resided in a monastery which later served many purposes, including being an assembly point for the Pilgrim Fathers.

At the turn of the eighteenth century, the Black Friars monastery became the home of Plymouth Gin. Part of the original building, the Refectory, is still intact and is protected as a national monument. The roof has been carefully restored, and an impressive collection of eighteenth-century prints now lines the walls.

Plymouth Gin has been distilled and bottled in these rather splendid surroundings ever since 1793. As gins go, it is notably dry, but soft, and the fresh water from the Devon streams is said to be responsible for this. As well as the traditional juniper berries, Plymouth Gin is made from English coriander seed, angelica root, sweet orange peel, orris root, lemon peel, and cardamon seed. When it first leaves the huge distilling tank it is a staggering 160 per cent proof but is watered down to 70 per cent proof before being bottled. Visitors to Black Friars are welcomed and further details can be obtained from Coates & Co (Plymouth) Ltd, Black Friars Distillery, Southside Street, Plymouth, Devon.

PONTEFRACT

Pontefract Cakes

The Romans used to grow liquorice plants in Pontefract, West Yorkshire, and habitually chewed the sweet roots, but local legend claims that liquorice roots were first grown by a Pontefract schoolmaster in the late sixteenth century. According to folklore, he found a bundle of the roots strewn on the beach – apparently washed ashore from a wrecked Armada galleon. As they were quite stout he thought that they would be useful for caning disruptive pupils at his school. The unfortunate boys who had to suffer this painful punishment took to chewing other, smaller roots, to distract their minds from the agony. Later, small cakes of liquorice were made for medicinal purposes and it was not until 1760 that a local chemist, George Dunhill, thought of adding sugar to the liquorice to make the round sweets with which we are familiar today.

In Pontefract there are at least five manufacturers producing Pontefract Cakes, and various other sweet-makers include them with their other products.

PRISTON MILL

Wholewheat Flour

Priston Mill gives a picture of old England, about four miles south of Bath, just off the Radstock Road. Until you have been there, it is difficult to believe that such places still exist.

An iron water-wheel, which is about 110 years old, is in daily use, working faithfully to provide power for the mill. Corn is ground by the age-old method between grindstones to provide fodder for the farm's dairy herd, and wholewheat flour for human consumption. There is a small farm shop where you can buy local crafts and tempting preserves, as well as Priston Mill's own wholewheat flour, bread, porridge oats and cookies.

These two old country recipes are greatly enhanced by the use of the nutty, wholewheat flour.

Wholewheat Bread (Makes 2 loaves)

1 pint (560ml) milk and water – about half and half
1 level tbsp dried yeast
1 level tbsp golden syrup
2lb (900g) stone ground, wholewheat flour
3 level tsp salt

Warm the milk and water to 110°F (45°C) (hand hot), remove from heat, and stir in syrup and yeast. Leave in a warm place until it becomes frothy. Mix enough of the yeast liquid into the flour and salt to make a softish, slightly powdery dough. Knead for 5min. Put in a bowl, cover, and leave in a warm place to double in size. Knead again for 5–10min. Grease 2 loaf tins and divide the dough between them so that each tin is approximately ⅔ full. Cover with polythene and leave to rise above the sides of the tin. Brush with a little milk and bake in an oven preheated to 450°F (230°C; Gas mark 8) for about 40min. To check whether they are sufficiently baked, tap the tins underneath. When ready, they sound hollow. One word of warning – addiction to crusty bread makes the soggy, white stuff somewhat un-desirable!

Wholewheat Cookies (Makes about 12)

8oz (225g) wholewheat flour
½tsp salt
1 rounded tsp each of mixed spice, cinnamon, ginger
2tsp baking powder
1½oz (42g) butter
3oz (84g) brown sugar
1 beaten egg
5tbsp milk (approx)

Preheat oven to 450°F (230°C; Gas mark 8). Mix the flour, salt, spices and baking powder in a bowl. Rub in the butter.

Add the sugar. Mix to a soft, but not sticky, dough with the beaten egg and sufficient milk. Roll out on a floured board to ¼in or slightly thicker. Cut into rounds with a 3in cutter. Bake on a baking tray for 12–15min, until well browned. They keep well in a tin and are especially good toasted with honey and butter.

RICHMOND

Maids of Honour were first made in the royal kitchens at Richmond Palace when Henry VIII was on the throne. The king happened to taste a pastry while he was touring the kitchens and liked it so much that he ordered the girl cook, responsible for the recipe, to produce 'Maids of Honour' as he called them, exclusively for him, for the rest of her life. So the poor girl was imprisoned. Her only visitor was Mr Billet, who supplied the ingredients for the cakes, and he eventually managed to learn the recipe from her.

After the girl's death, Mr Billet opened a Maids of Honour shop in Richmond. The business and the secret recipe was kept in the Billet family for many generations. A Mr Newens, great-great-grandfather of the present proprietor of the Newen's Maids of Honour Shop, went to work in Mr Billet's shop and is said to have purchased the secret recipe for a thousand guineas, and subsequently opened his own shop in Richmond. Later he moved to 288, Kew Road, Kew Gardens, where the establishment still stands today, and where, to the best of Mr P. J. Newen's knowledge, 'the cakes we now make are identical in every way to the original recipe (still made entirely by hand)'. The following recipe is a popular one, but is not the original – I do not think I could afford the thousand guineas for that!

Richmond Maids of Honour   (Makes 8–12)

1 pint (560ml) milk
2 level tbsp sugar
1tsp rennet
8oz (225g) puff pastry

3oz (84g) butter
1 large egg or 2 small ones
1tbsp brandy
½oz (14g) ground almonds

Heat the milk with 1tbsp of sugar, until it is just warm, not hot, to touch. Overheating will prevent the rennet from working. Remove from heat and add the rennet. Stir for half a minute only and leave for about half an hour to set. Transfer the junket to a very fine sieve, stand over a bowl, and leave overnight. Preheat oven to 425°F (220°C; Gas mark 7), and lightly grease some small, deep cake tins. This recipe makes 8–12 cakes depending on tin size. Roll out pastry and line the tins. Mash the butter to soften, and mix with the curds. Beat the egg with the brandy, almonds, remaining sugar, and mix into curds and butter. Spoon the mixture into pastry cases, half filling each. Bake for 18–20 min. The filling will rise considerably during cooking and subside on cooling.

There is an interesting row of houses facing onto the west side of Richmond Green. These rather quaint historic houses – known as Maids of Honour Row – were built for the ladies of the Court, during the reign of George I.

RIPON

Ripon is a small market town in Yorkshire with a great cathedral dedicated to St Wilfrid. A hornblower in traditional costume still blows an old horn each evening at the market cross, to maintain a colourful old tradition. But it is the patron saint of the cathedral who is responsible for some of Ripon's traditional recipes.

Every August Bank holiday, the inhabitants of Ripon celebrate the feast day of St Wilfrid. There are a few folk who still rise as early as 4am to bake little jam and lemon cheese tarts, called Wilfra Tarts, which are put by the front door on huge old meat dishes. Traditionally, passers-by are invited to help themselves.

Wilfra Tarts

1lb (450g) shortcrust pastry
Jam
LEMON CHEESE
2oz (56g) butter
4oz (112g) sugar
1 egg, beaten
Grated rind and juice of 1 lemon

Roll out the pastry and line as many greased patty tins as possible. Fill half with jam. Make the lemon cheese by creaming the butter and sugar together, and then mixing in the egg, rind and juice. Use this to fill the rest of the pastry cases. Bake in an oven at 450°F (230°C; Gas mark 8) for about 10min, until the lemon filling is set and the pastry lightly browned.

Ripon Spice Bread is another local speciality and several old versions of the recipe simply instruct one to work a little lard into some risen bread dough, along with currants, raisins, and spices. This recipe is based on a more explicit one, originally calling for 3½lb (1.5kg) of flour.

Ripon Spice Bread

1lb (450g) flour
Pinch salt
1tsp (or more) mixed spice
2oz (56g) butter
2oz (56g) lard
4oz (112g) sugar
4oz (112g) currants
4oz (112g) raisins
1tbsp peel, chopped
1 egg
¾oz (21g) fresh yeast and 1tsp sugar
Warm milk

Sieve the flour, salt and spice together and rub in the butter and lard. Mix in sugar, raisins, currants and peel. Fork mix the egg and add as well. Cream the fresh yeast with 1tsp of sugar and a little warm milk, and add this, with sufficient warm milk to make a not too sticky dough. Cover and leave to rise until doubled in bulk. Knead for a bit on a floured board and then ease into a 2lb loaf tin. Leave to prove for another 15min and then bake at 400°F (200°C; Gas mark 6) for about 1hr.

Spice Bread was often made at Christmas time when it was called Yule Bread. It was served to casual droppers-in with chunks of cheese and warming, mulled ale, and was made in other parts of Yorkshire too.

SAFFRON WALDEN

'The Saffron of England is the most excellent of all other . . .'

(Holinshed)

Saffron

Saffron Walden, a historically rich town in Essex, owes much of its past prosperity to the crocus, from which the valuable powder saffron is extracted. Crocuses were once grown in abundance in the fields around old Walden, and this eventually led to the town being known as Saffron Walden. However, no saffron is produced in or around the market town these days – the trade in fact died towards the end of the eighteenth century. It would hardly be an economic proposition to grow saffron now since it takes over 4,000 crocus flowers to produce 1oz of saffron! It is frequently claimed to be the most expensive spice in the world. Even in the sixteenth century, it was sold, according to Thomas Tusser, 'at twenty shillings [£1] a pound'.

Legend has it that the first crocus bulb to be smuggled into England came from its native Arabia (where it was called zaffer) concealed in the palmer's staff of a pilgrim in Edward III's reign. Saffron was used by the ancient Romans and Greeks to make perfume, and in the East, and in due course in parts of Britain, its properties were considered invaluable in medicinal folklore. Even as recently as 1921, there was a reference, by a witness in court at Poplar in East London, to a saffron tea, laced with brandy, for curing measles. Saffron was also used as a natural dye, and of course in cookery. However the people of Saffron Walden did not seem to like saffron flavouring very much as there is virtually no reference to their having used it to enhance their foods.

But to the north, in the neighbouring county of Suffolk, where much Essex saffron was sold, Suffolk Saffron Buns (see Suffolk section) were very popular.

ST ALBAN'S

Popladys or Pope Ladies

On New Year's Day in St Alban's in Hertfordshire, dough cakes known as Popladys or Pope Ladies were once hawked in the street by boys and girls, and were sold in every baker's shop. They were vaguely connected with an obscure myth about Pope Joan but their origin is unknown. A Poplady was described in 1820 in the *Gentlemen's Magazine*, vol 190.

> It was a plain cake, like the cross buns sold on Good Friday, but, instead of being circular, was long and narrow, rudely resembling the human figure, with two dried raisins or currants to represent eyes and another for the mouth, the lower part being formed rather like the outer case of an Egyptian mummy.

A Hertfordshire correspondent adds that 'the little figures were very highly glazed with a brushing of milk and sugar so they came out very brown and shiny'. Popladys were still in existence earlier this century – made by the local Bugler family – but there is no trace of them today.

ST BRIAVEL'S

Bread and Cheese Dole

> 'Bachelor's fare: bread and cheese, and kisses.'
> (Jonathan Swift (1667-1745) in *Polite Conversation*)

A Bread and Cheese dole is distributed at St Briavel's Church in Gloucestershire, every Whit Sunday after the evening service. The earliest mention of the custom is recorded in a Gloucestershire history book of 1799. The origin of the dole is somewhat obscure, but local folklore informs us that it commemorates the villagers' right to collect firewood and graze animals on a local acreage of land known as the Hudnalls. This privilege was only granted by King John after the courageous Countess of Hereford emulated Lady Godiva, so it is alleged, by riding through the village naked.

Actually, I have a very descriptive leaflet about the dole, issued by St Briavel's, and my sincere thanks go to the charming vicar who scrawled: 'Much of this is inaccurate –

stick to the first paragraph' at the conclusion of the text. I am most grateful – just think of all the fibs I might have told you!

SANDWICH

Sandwiches

The town of Sandwich in Kent was one of the original Cinque Ports, and according to legend, the 4th Earl of Sandwich, John Montagu (1718–92) was responsible for naming the much favoured British snack food. The Earl, so the story goes, was so fond of playing at the card table that he could not tear himself away for meals. His servant apparently prevented him from starving by bringing him food sandwiched between two pieces of bread, and the Earl was able to munch away without interrupting his game. Ham sandwiches are quite popular for picnics, and believe it or not, a small town near Sandwich is called Ham.

SCONE

Before the Union of Scotland and England the Kings of Scotland were always crowned at Scone in Perthshire, and many people like to link the town with the tea-time scones. This culinary association, however, is unlikely to be very sound. Etymologists prefer to derive the name scone from the Gaelic *sgonn* – a mouthful or mass – or from the Dutch *schoonbrot* – fine bread. The Scottish scone, pronounced skonn, differs from Devon scones (or splits) in that it is generally cooked on a griddle rather than in the oven.

Scones (Makes 2)

8oz (225g) flour
½tsp bicarbonate of soda
½tsp cream of tartar
Good pinch salt
Sour milk

Sieve all the dry ingredients together and pour in sufficient sour milk to make a soft dough. Turn onto a floured board, divide, and knead into 2 rounds. Roll out each one to about ¼in thick, more if you prefer thicker scones. Mark each round into quarters with a sharp knife, but do not cut right through the dough. Heat an oiled griddle, or thick frying pan, until flour will brown in a few seconds, and then cook the scones, both sides, until pale brown. Wrap in a clean towel until cool, to keep the crusts soft. Serve the scones, in quarters, split and buttered.

SHETLAND ISLES

There are some hundred or so of the Shetland Isles scattered off the north-east coast of Scotland. They are remote and wild, and the majority are uninhabited. The cooks there, like those in the rest of Scotland, make excellent shortbread, and a large round shortbread cake was an attraction at local weddings. It was customarily marked into pieces, and a sweet was placed on the middle section. Each unmarried guest was invited to break off a piece of the shortbread, and woe betide anyone whose fingers happened to touch the sweet. Such careless action prophesied spinsterhood or bachelorhood for the clumsy one. The cool climate in the Shetlands is ideal for making shortbread as the dough tends to become oily and tough when worked in warm weather.

Shortbread

5oz (140g) butter
2oz (56g) caster sugar
7oz (196g) plain flour
1oz (28g) rice flour
Caraway seeds (optional)

First blend the butter and sugar together with as little working as possible, to avoid oiliness, in a bowl. Gradually work in the flours, and caraway seeds if you like them, to make a dough. (Incidentally, the seeds are claimed to aid digestion greatly by medicinal folklorists.) Gently press the dough into a shortbread mould which has been lightly greased and floured, or use a 7in sandwich tin, and invert the shortbread onto a prepared baking sheet, taking care to keep the design whole. Real Scottish shortbread is made about ¾in thick – thicker and much better, in my opinion, than commercial shortbread – and this takes about 45–60min to brown in an oven set at 325°F (170°C; Gas mark 3). Leave to cool on the baking sheet otherwise it will crumble and the moulded pattern will be spoilt. If you have no wooden mould, decorate the uncooked cake by crimping the edges and forking some sort of pattern in the middle.

SHREWSBURY

Shrewsbury is situated in a horseshoe bend made by the River Severn on the doorstep to Wales. This Shropshire town has many medieval buildings jumbled happily in curiously named streets like Grope Lane, Dogpol, Gullet Passage and Butcher Row.

The town's most prominent fare – Shrewsbury Biscuits – used to be called Shrewsbury or Shroesbury Cakes, and existed in the sixteenth century. It was customary to give Shrewsbury Cakes to famous personnages who visited the town, and at one time the cakes were also eaten at funeral feasts. The most famous maker of Shrewsbury Cakes was Palin, whose circular trademark of 'Palin's Original Shrewsbury Cakes', showing the three loggerheads of the borough arms, was created by Thomas Plummer in 1875.

Shrewsbury Biscuits

4oz (112g) butter
4oz (112g) caster sugar
1 medium egg
8oz (225g) plain flour
Grated rind of 1 lemon
½oz (14g) caraway seeds or 2oz (56g) currants
Sugar for sprinkling

Cream the butter with the sugar until light and fluffy. Beat the egg and add to the creamed mix. Stir in the flour and grated rind, and mix to a stiff paste. The biscuits can be made plain but taste better if a flavouring is added. Caraway seeds were once popular, and are worth trying for a change. However, currants are more popular today. Work in the chosen flavouring and turn the paste onto a floured board. Roll out, not too thinly, and cut 2½in rounds, using a fluted cutter. Sprinkle with sugar, preferably caster, and place on a non-stick baking tray. Bake in an oven preheated to 350°F (180°C; Gas mark 4) for 15–18min, until pale brown.

Shrewsbury Biscuits are no longer made commercially in the town but Yorkshire Biscuits Ltd, a firm started in 1959 making 'hand-baked biscuits from home recipes', distributes the Shropshire specialities all over the country with great success.

SHROPSHIRE

In the last century it was customary to go a-souling on All Souls' Day (2 November) or on the eve of the same, All Saints' Day (1 November). This practice was also observed in several other counties, Cheshire and Yorkshire for instance, but was not common in the south of England.

> Soul, soul, for a soul-cake,
> Pray good missus, a soul-cake,
> One for Peter, two for Paul.

Children used to chant this jingle as they knocked on people's doors begging for soul-cakes. These were in fact any gift given on this day – fruit, drink, money or little plain or fruit buns. This old recipe is attributed to Mrs Durant, late of Tong Castle, and is taken from *Bye-Gones relating to Wales and the Border Countries* (1909–10).

Soul-Cakes

2lb (900g) flour
4oz (112g) butter
8oz (225g) sugar
2 eggs
2tbsp barm
Spice
Saffron
Milk to make it into a soft dough

Put all the ingredients together, except the sugar and spice and let the mixture be left before the fire for half an hour; then add the sugar and spice, mix well, make into flat cakes, mark each one and bake.

SNOWDONIA

The beautiful, yet complex Snowdonia mountain range is found in the Welsh county of Gwynedd. Snowdon, the highest peak, towers majestically up to 3,560ft above sea level, making it the highest mountain in England and Wales.

Eagles are frequently associated with the mountain. The Welsh call Snowdon and the smaller, adjacent mountains,

Eryri, which means an abode of eagles. Some people used to believe that if eagles were seen circling high above the mountain's summit, Wales would soon have a victory, but if the birds were seen flying low over the rocks, defeat would not be far away. If they were heard crying for any length of time, some tragedy was predicted.

Snowdon Pudding or Eagle's Abode Pudding (Pwdin Eryri) was originally served to travellers who patronised a hotel at the foot of Snowdon. It is, I suppose, somewhat reminiscent of the mountain, when turned out on a plate and brought to the table still with the steam resembling the summer mists which hover persistently above the peak. Maybe the unknown creator was attempting to simulate the mountain's dark nooks and crannies when they decided to stud the pudding with raisins!

Snowdon Pudding (Serves 6)

Butter
3oz (84g) raisins (approx)
8oz (225g) shredded suet
8oz (225g) breadcrumbs
2oz (56g) cornflour
1 level tsp salt
6oz (168g) lemon marmalade
Grated rind of 1 lemon
6oz (168g) brown sugar
6 eggs, beaten

First take a fancy 2 pint pudding mould and butter it generously. Stone the raisins but do not chop them. Stick them to the inside of the mould in little clusters. Combine all the remaining ingredients in a bowl and spoon into the raisin studded bowl, being careful not to dislodge the fruit. Cover with foil and tie securely. Immerse the bottom half of the mould in a pan of boiling water and cook for about 1½hr. The pudding should be turned out and served steaming hot, accompanied with cream, custard or a sweet sauce. If only half quantity is required, use a pint size mould and cook for about 50min.

SOMERSET

On St James' Day [25 July] the apples are christened.
(Old Somerset Saying)

Scrumpy

The name Somerset is derived from Old English and means the county of the summer farm dwellers. Somerset scrumpy is farmhouse cider, the traditional drink of the county's inhabitants from time immemorial. There is no other drink quite like it – commercial cider is entirely different. Scrumpy is similar to dry white wine and is extremely potent – the name comes from the Hebrew word *shekar*, meaning strong drink. It is still made locally and sold in Somerset villages in flasks and earthenware pots.

I am indebted to Edgar Purton of Winslade Farmhouse who kindly took many pains to explain scrumpy-making to me. He says: 'Locally scrumpy is made by just chopping up the apples, building a "cheese" with wheat straw, catching the juice, and letting it ferment'. Mr Purton's neighbours make about 300 gallons a year, for their own use, drinking several pints a day when working! According to Mr Purton's account, the 'cheese' generally consists of

8 or 9 layers each of chopped apples and straw. It stands in a heavy tray, on a concrete block, with an outlet to let the juice run into a half-barrel. The cheese's own weight is sufficient for a day, then the plate over the top is wound down by means of the wheel (with teeth in it) on a screw from up in the loft above. The sides of the cheese are pared away as the cheese is crushed – taking two or three days to do this – and when it is about a foot square it is scrapped and another cheese started. The straw is the best wheat straw if possible, and the apples are Morgans, as they come first and are plentiful, then fallen Bramleys (it does not matter if they are brown and a bit rotten). The good Bramleys are stored to last until Easter, for eating. The red, small, cider apples come later on, and I have known cider making in January! Of course, it takes a lot of apples, and the old

waggon is used, towed behind the tractor, for picking. About three or four waggon loads would be a rather good year on average.

Mr Purton emphasies that the apples are not treated in any way, but are only pure apple juice 'lovely the first two days, a drastic medicine on the third and fourth perhaps, and then they have fermented enough to be called cider, though it is still unwise to drink much'. Mr Purton also recalls reading in *The Countryman* some years ago of a farmer who shovelled up the cow-muck with the apples, and when accosted said that it made them work better!

Wassailing

In several towns in Somerset the apple trees are still cere-moniously wassailed on the old Twelfth Night – 17 January. This custom stems from the rites practised by farmers in days gone by, to ward off the evil spirits at this time of year, and thus prevent them from harming the crops. The word wassail is derived from the Anglo-Saxon greeting *Was hail* meaning 'Your good health'. At Carhampton, and other places, the locals gather round one of the prime trees and scrumpy is poured over the tree's roots. Pieces of toast are strung on the branches, to appease the good spirits, and the traditional invocation is sung:

> Here's to thee, old apple tree,
> Whence thou may'st bud
> And whence thou may'st blow,
> And whence thou may'st bear apples enow;
> Hats full, caps full,
> And our pockets full too.
> Huzza! Huzza! Huzza!

Incidentally, the old wassail bowls always had pieces of toast floating in them and here lies the origin of our custom of drinking people's health – toasting.

Apples are used for Somerset Apple Cake as well as for making scrumpy. This is very quickly mixed – in fact so roughly that one is always amazed when it emerges from the oven looking so good.

Somerset Apple Cake

8oz (225g) self-raising flour
Pinch salt
2oz (56g) granulated sugar
1 large cooking apple, peeled and cored (eg, Bramley)
1oz (28g) lard
1 egg
Water
Brown sugar

Mix the flour, salt and sugar together. Roughly chop the apple and lard and stir in with the egg. Add enough water to make a solid mass that leaves the sides of the bowl clean. Heap into a round tin (7in or 8in) which has been greased and lined. Sprinkle with brown sugar. Bake at 350°F (180°C; Gas mark 4) for about 1hr.

SOUTHEND-ON-SEA

The longest pleasure pier in the world is at Southend-on-Sea in Essex, and its fame rather overshadows that of the modest, yet flourishing whitebait fishing industry. In fact, many residents are quite surprised to hear that one exists. Whitebait are, of course, the small fry of herring and sprats, and thrive particularly well in estuaries, as at Southend. Previously they were found further up the River Thames towards London, but water pollution has now curtailed their existence there.

They should be eaten as soon as possible after they are caught; a silvery sheen which dulls with age, determines their condition.

Southend Whitebait

First turn them into a sieve and coat with flour. Then transfer to a chip basket and immerse in hot oil, heated to at least 400°F (200°C). Cook for 2–3min. Shake off excess oil and serve in a folded napkin with salt and brown bread and butter, garnished with a lemon wedge.

Blessing the Catch

A service which was revived by Southend Chamber of Trade in the 1930s takes place annually at the end of September. This is known as the 'Blessing of the Catch', and, weather permitting, several ministers conduct a short service from a trawler, at the end of the pier.

The service is followed by a whitebait buffet and later, in November, by a grand Whitebait Festival; an elaborate feast held in a banquet suite in the town. Originally this festival took place on the same day as the 'Blessing of the Catch', but the separation was advised by wise men in the Chamber of Trade as it was considered that the two events on one day were possibly 'gastronomically overwhelming'.

STILTON

Stilton Cheese

'The King of English Cheese' is Stilton; very few would dispute this. Its distinct, unforgettable flavour has been sought to complete grand banquets for the last two centuries. There was a time when only the privileged few could afford the delicacy, but happily, with the vastly improved manufacturing processes, Stilton is now in plentiful supply, available all over the country, and within most people's pockets.

When this blue-veined cheese was first made it was called Lady Beaumont's cheese as it was developed by her housekeeper at Quenby Hall sometime in the early eighteenth century. The housekeeper also taught the art to one of Lady Beaumont's daughters, who later became Mrs Paulet when she married Farmer Paulet from Wymondham, near Melton Mowbray. Mrs Paulet supplied her sister, who married Cooper Thornhill, with cheeses to sell in their Bell Inn in Stilton. For a while Lady Beaumont's cheese was named English Parmesan and then, as people who frequented the Bell Inn and sampled the cheese told their friends about it, it understandably became known as Stilton cheese.

Mrs Paulet's method of making Silton remained in use until the beginning of this century. Unfortunately, the operation was risky and laborious, resulting in much waste of both cheese and labour. The cheeses took eighteen months to mature, but nowadays, with regulated temperatures in modern dairies, only four months are needed.

To make a 14lb cheese, 17 gallons of milk are required. The milk is poured into cheese vats with a 'starter' to form the curds, and then cut, stirred, and drained twice. Next the curds are salted and weighed, and from then on are regarded as cheeses. They are shaped, wrapped in clean cloths, and left in a cool, humid atmosphere to encourage the familiar, rough coat to form. Then they are taken to maturing rooms where they are pierced to allow air to enter them, so that mould can grow. Thus one can see that Stilton making is a quite natural process; the blue veins are not, as many people think, a manufactured addition to flavour the cheese.

White Stilton, a less common but nevertheless very acceptable cheese, is simply young Stilton which has not matured long enough for the veins to grow.

Many people have tried to imitate Stilton, and in 1969 a High Court order was passed to protect the Stilton name. There is also a Stilton Cheese Makers Association who advise their members, and promote their very special product. Stilton is still very regional and is only produced in the East Midlands.

When serving Stilton, you should not use a scoop. This, according to residents of Melton Mowbray, is a very wasteful practice. In fact they have a popular saying, 'Cut high, cut low, cut level'; the idea is to cut across the top of the cheese, leaving the surface flat as before.

If you travel north up the A1, the Great North Road, you can still turn off left into Stilton. The Bell Inn? Yes, it is still there but sadly is no longer open, and has become a little neglected. According to a Stiltonian there is some sort of preservation order on it, but at time of writing any active restoration is dormant. However, travellers need not continue on their way unrefreshed, for further up the road there is another pub – the Stilton Cheese – where you can soak up your drink with as much Stilton as you want.

SUFFOLK

Saffron Buns were more popular in Suffolk than in neighbouring Essex, from where the saffron invariably came. Some reports suggest that ships docking at Suffolk ports after their journey up from the Cornish coast helped to popularise saffron flavouring. An account in the *East Anglian Times* dated 21 March 1951, recorded that people in Lowestoft still enjoyed their saffron buns, rather than the hot-cross buns enjoyed elsewhere, at Easter time. The saffron flour for these was obtained from Cornwall – the only other county in Britain which uses saffron in cooking to any significant degree. The buns' popularity has dwindled a bit of late, but no doubt will enjoy a revival one of these days.

Saffron Buns

1 dram (3½g) saffron
Little water, approx ½ gill (70ml)
1lb (450g) strong plain white flour
Pinch salt
3oz (84g) butter
3oz (84g) currants
1oz (28g) candied peel, chopped
2oz (56g) sugar
½oz (14g) fresh yeast
1tsp sugar
1½ gills (210ml) warm milk

Soak the saffron in a little water overnight. Sieve the flour and salt and rub in the butter. Mix in the currants, peel and sugar, and make a well. Stir the fresh yeast and 1tsp of sugar into the warm, not hot, milk, and pour with the yellow saffron water into the well to make a slackish dough. Cover and leave in a warmish place to double in size. Turn on to a floured board and knead for a few minutes. Shape into buns and place on a greased baking sheet, spacing well. Leave to prove again – about 20min. Bake at 425°F (220°C; Gas mark 7) for 10–12min and then remove from the oven. Brush with a glaze made with 1tbsp sugar dissolved in a little milk, and return to hot oven for another couple of minutes. Traditionally, the buns were eaten hot for breakfast on Good Friday.

Suffolk Rusks are quite plain little things – light and crumbly and good to nibble.

Suffolk Rusks

1lb (450g) self-raising flour
Pinch of salt
5oz (140g) butter
1 egg, beaten
2–3tbsp milk

Sieve the flour and salt together, and rub in the butter to make a breadcrumb-like mixture. Add the egg and sufficient milk to make a workable dough. Turn on to a floured board and roll out to ¾in thick. Cut 2in rounds and put on an oiled baking tray. Bake in an oven at 400°F (200°C; Gas mark 6) for 15min, then remove and split each rusk. Return to oven and bake until golden and crisp – taking another 15min.

Visitors passing through the Suffolk village of Woodbridge should be able to buy Suffolk Rusks at the Cake Shop, a local bakery in the main shopping area.

SUSSEX

Mead and Wines

The Merrydown Wine Company, now a very successful concern, was started about thirty years ago by three partners with a capital of £100 and no premises at all. The company took its now-famous name from a modest little cottage overlooking the valley below Rotherfield in Sussex. The winery at Horam in Sussex is now one of the most modern and efficient in the country. As well as the Honeymooners' Mead, and the versatile cider vinegar, Merrydown produce Apple, Gooseberry, Redcurrant, Whitecurrant, Bilberry, Elderberry, Morello Cherry, Raspberry, Blackberry and Orange Wines. The following drink recipes are taken from André Launay's *Merrydown Book of Country Wines*.

Merrydown Honeymooner

2 parts brandy
1 part Merrydown Mead
Shake with ice

Merrydown Fruit Cup

Steep a pound of strawberries or other fruit in 2 bottles of Merrydown Whitecurrant Wine and 2 liqueur glasses of brandy for at least 1hr before required. Before serving add ice and sugar to taste and finally one bottle of Champagne. Mix in a large bowl and serve with ladle.

Sussex has also named two suet puddings. The first, Blanket Pudding, is based on a recipe dating from the early nineteenth century.

Sussex Blanket Pudding (Serves 8–10)

12oz (337g) plain white flour
8oz (225g) fine stale white breadcrumbs
12oz (337g) shredded beef suet
Pinch salt
2 eggs, beaten
Little milk
Jam or golden syrup

Mix the flour, breadcrumbs, suet and salt together. Add the eggs and enough milk to make a light elastic dough. Roll out on a floured cloth to about ¼in thick. Spread with jam or syrup to within 1in of the edges. Wet the edges and roll the suet pastry up, like a swiss roll, by pulling the cloth up. Pinch and seal the edges and tie the roll in a floured cloth. Boil for about 2¼hr.

The second Sussex pudding is known by a variety of different names – Palm Pudding, because it was often made on Palm Sunday, and Pond or Well Pudding, because of the little 'pond' or 'well' of delectable sticky sweet sauce that squelches out of the pudding as soon as it is cut.

Sussex Palm, Pond or Well Pudding (Serves 8)

8oz (225g) flour
Good pinch of salt
4oz (112g) shredded suet
8oz (225g) currants
Water
4oz (112g) butter
4oz (112g) demerara sugar
Little milk

Mix the flour, salt, suet and currants with enough water to make an easy to roll dough. Turn onto a floured board and break into two pieces, one roughly twice the size of the other. Roll the larger piece into a round and leave on one side. Roll the smaller piece into a round also. Cream the butter with the sugar and pile into the centre of the small round. Pinch the edges in an attempt to enclose the butter and sugar mix. Invert the suet ball on the larger round. Pinch up the edges to enclose it and seal with water. Tie in a floured cloth and boil for 3hr.

SWALEDALE

A hard, dark, treacle toffee is a Guy Fawkes night sweetmeat from Swaledale in Yorkshire, and is traditionally crunched whilst standing round the bonfire.

Swaledale Toffee or Tom Trot

8oz (225g) brown sugar
8oz (225g) treacle
4oz (112g) butter

Melt all the ingredients in a pan over a low heat. Simmer for about half an hour, until it reaches crack stage, ie 290–300°F (143–150°C). Pour into buttered tins and when nearly cool, mark into squares. Or, if you like sticky tangles, pour it onto a cold slab, and as soon as you can bear to handle it, pull it into long ropes, twisting as you go. If a slightly lighter toffee is preferred, golden syrup can be substituted for half the treacle.

TAIN

Cheeses

Tain is an ancient Royal Burgh of Easter Ross, situated on the blue Dornoch Firth in Scotland, and apart from James IV's many pilgrimages to the town, it now deserves recognition for its cheese creamery, which was only started just over a decade ago. Reggie Stone recalled the crowdie he used to eat, spread on oatcakes, long ago, and Susannah Stone promptly obliged and made some. Although it was a success with her family, Susannah found that she had made too much for them to eat and so she took the remains to a local grocer, Hector Ross. Not surprisingly, the Tain grocer asked Susannah to make some more, and in no time at all 'Highland Fine' cheeses were in business.

Dating back to the time of the ancient Picts, the making of Highland Crowdie is a fine old Scottish craft, and yet is one of the simplest ways of making cheese from drained milk curds. It bears a certain similarity to the cottage cheese made in England, but is more delicately flavoured. The Stones also mix their Crowdie with double cream – 2 parts crowdie to 1 of cream – and with wild garlic. Finely chopped leaves of the latter are blended with cream to make the aromatic, fresh tasting Hramsa. The local Scottish wild garlic imparts a much lighter oniony flavour than ordinary garlic, and does not leave the breath tainted. Local rumour has it that this variety of garlic will cure numerous ailments from heart disease to asthma and in Celtic lore, it is regarded as the 'all healing herb'. An old Mohammedan legend, however, is not so kind to garlic in general. It declares that when Satan came out of the Garden of Eden, after the fall of man, garlic sprang from under his left foot and onion from beneath his right!

The Stones at Tain also make a very excellent Double Cream Cheese, fit for any laird's table, and a most unusual cream cheese, rolled in toasted pinhead oatmeal, called Caboc. The latter is made according to an old recipe of Susannah's family which 'from mother to daughter, has descended from Mariota, the romantic daughter of the fifteenth century Macdonald of the Isles'. It was originally made for the Chieftain but thanks to the Stones, it can now be enjoyed throughout Britian by everybody.

TEWKESBURY

Mustard

The writer of *Topographical Excursion in the year 1634* wrote, 'we had not the will to go out of our way to be bit by the nose at Tewkesbury, but left it on our left'. This was the author's way of describing the extreme pungency of old Tewkesbury Mustard. Similarly, Shakespeare in his *King Henry the Fourth*, makes a reference to the same condiment, with Falstaff's simile, 'his wit is as thick as Tewkesbury mustard'. There is also the old English proverb, describing a pert fellow, 'He looks as if he lives on Tewkesbury mustard'. Thus the Gloucestershire town has quite a reputation to live up to, but alas, there is not much mustard made in the town nowadays although some is still available.

In the past, wild mustard grew profusely around Tewkesbury, for the soil in this area apparently suited it very well. Up to the year 1720 the mustard was prepared in a very rough fashion. The seeds were pounded with a pestle and mortar – often the pestle was a cannon ball and the mortar was made of iron – and mixed with strong vinegar, wine or ale and horse-radish, the latter being supposed to impart extra strength to the mustard. This pounding was quite terrifying and often likened, in old chronicles, to the sound of angry thunder. In fact in the theatre, the pestle and mortar were frequently utilised to mimic thunderstorms.

The coarsely prepared mustard was said to be splendid for clearing the head. Fuller confirms this in his *Worthies of England* (1662) and also tells a popular story of his era, concerning two servants, in which each man wishes to conceive his master superior to the other's. ' "My master", saith the one, "spends more in mustard than thine does in beef". Whereunto the other returned, "The more saucy men his followers".'

TIPTREE

Strawberries

Curly locks, curly locks,
Wilt thou be mine?
Thou shalt not wash dishes, nor yet feed the swine,
But sit on a cushion and sew a fine seam,
And feed upon strawberries, sugar and cream.
(Trad nursery rhyme)

The name Tiptree, to any Essex resident, immediately conjures up a picture of juicy red strawberries growing profusely in numerous strawberry fields. If you happen to be in there at the right time of year (late May to July), you can go and pick them for yourself, as many farmers now cultivate several strawberry fields solely for the general public to harvest. If you pick enough, you might get a chance to try this traditional recipe and still have some to smother with sugar and cream for tea.

Strawberry Jam

2½lb (1.125kg) strawberries (choose small, firm fruit)
2tbsp lemon juice
2lb (900g) preserving sugar

I find that the smaller strawberries are better for making jam as they do not take so long to cook and therefore keep their shape better. Alas, these small fruit take much longer to pick. Wash and hull the berries and put them in a large pan, preferably a preserving pan, with the lemon juice but no extra liquid. Simmer until the strawberries soften but do not let them go mushy. This takes from 10–20min, depending on the size of the fruit used. Add the sugar and stir carefully to encourage it to dissolve. Then bring to the boil and boil rapidly until setting point is reached. Test this by dropping a teaspoon of the jam onto a saucer and letting it cool. If it wrinkles when you rub your finger over it, setting point has been reached. Remove the pan from the heat immediately and leave to cool for about 15min. Transfer the jam to clean jars, cover and label.

If you are not able to gather your own strawberries you can still eat jam made with Tiptree strawberries. Wilkin & Sons have been selling their 'Tiptree' (registered trade mark) Strawberry Conserve for nearly a century. The business was started by the present Mr Wilkin's grandfather in 1864. In those early days Mr Wilkin was only concerned with growing strawberries and was one of the first people to do so. He was quite a pioneer, encouraging the other local folk to grow the fruit too, and arranged for the fruit to be sent to London to be sampled in the very best establishments. The pickers would rise before daybreak and work fiendishly for a couple of hours. The berries were then transported by train, to arrive in the London hotels in time for breakfast. After several years, an Australian friend suggested that Mr Wilkin should try his hand at jam making. He took up the challenge and in 1885 established the jam factory that was to become so famous. In the beginning, the premises consisted of one small room and a modest chimney. The present Mr Wilkin recalls his grandfather telling him how he once had to sell a horse in order to pay the week's wages!

Today Wilkin's jams are exported all over the world; even the Chinese are partial to the odd dollop of strawberry conserve – I noticed a consignment labelled for Hong Kong when I visited the factory. Of all the preserves that Wilkin & Sons produce, the strawberry varieties remain the most popular.

Incidentally, at time of writing, Wilkin & Sons are offering caravan holidays in the Essex countryside in return for so many hours of strawberry picking. Enquiries to Wilkin & Sons, Tiptree, Colchester, Essex.

TUNBRIDGE WELLS

Tunbridge Wells is situated on the borders of Kent and Sussex and has certain Bathonian characteristics. The name Wells, of course, suggests watery connections, and the Chalybeate Spring, with its health-giving properties, can still be seen today in the famous, tree-lined Pantiles.

Wafers

Tunbridge Wells Wafers, or Romary Biscuits, seem to be the town's only culinary attribute. Alfred Romary, the son of a humble weaver, decided against following in his father's footsteps and opened a bakery at 26, Church Road, Tunbridge Wells, in 1862. In addition to the usual bakery sales, he introduced a lacy, paper-thin biscuit which was considered to be the perfect accompaniment to wine. As wine was then a daily drink among the 'best people' the wafer soon became popular, and its fame spread to the London clubs. Queen Victoria was a customer when she visited the town in 1872 and the Romary family still treasure the gold sovereign that accompanied her order. The oven at 26, Church Road was set in brickwork in the chimney. Wood was burnt inside it, in order to raise the temperature, and then the wafers were baked by the heat retained in the bricks. This enterprising oven has been scrapped in favour of more modern machinery, and A. Romary & Co Ltd has become an associate of Rowntrees. The company is still thriving in Glasgow, believe it or not, and produces a fair number of Tunbridge Wells Wafers which are on sale throughout the country, in the smaller, specialist food shops. The wafers are about 3in in diameter, very delicate and lacy, and are good with cheese as well as wine.

TWEEDMOUTH

Tweedmouth Feast and Salmon

Although administratively part of Berwick-on-Tweed, the border town of Tweedmouth remains distinctive for its old custom known as the Tweedmouth Feast Week. The feast started some 1,000 years ago as a patronal festival of the Church, and a trade fair developed simultaneously with it. When the coastal railway was built, Tweedmouth lost much of its importance and trade. However in the 1940s, the feast was given a new lease of life when the medieval style Master of the Revels was replaced by a Salmon Queen – to signify the importance of the ancient occupation of fishing for salmon in this area.

The revellers of the past used to call their elaborate tea parties 'Salmon Kettles', and the main fare at these functions was of course salmon, followed traditionally by Gooseberry Tart to an old Northumberland recipe.

Nowadays the feast runs for a week in late July and follows modern carnival lines with entertainments such as sticky bun-eating races, and torchlight processions. The Salmon supper still takes place at the beginning of the Feast Week, but the Gooseberry Tart seems to have been forgotten. A local recipe for 'crimping' salmon, sent by a Berwick librarian, reads as follows:

> The fresh salmon is split up the back and cut into portions suitable for one person. I pound of salt is put in water, sufficient to cover the fish, and brought to the boil. The fish is then immersed and the water skimmed. It must not be allowed to remain in the water for longer than 6 minutes, or once the water has come to the boil again. A little of the water in which the salmon is poached – called dover – makes an excellent sauce.

URCHFONT

Urchfont Mustard

The Wiltshire Tracklement Company Ltd at 44, Church Street, Calne, in Wiltshire, produces a distinctive tracklement, Urchfont Mustard, which takes its name from a charming Wiltshire village. The proprietors, the Tullbergs, also have a restaurant, Maslen's, in Calne, and Helen Tullberg is responsible for creating many local recipes, one of which appears below.

Pork Chops with Urchfont Cheese

Grill some pork chops in your usual way. Meanwhile grate 2oz (56g) Gruyère or Emmental cheese and mix to a thick paste with equal quantities of Urchfont Mustard and cream. Spread this on one side of the chops and replace under grill till bubbling hot.

WAKEFIELD

The recipe below, named after the West Yorkshire city of Wakefield, is a variation of the old-fashioned English Summer Pudding which is made with different fruits in different areas.

Wakefield Apple Pudding   (Serves 4–6)

1½lb (675g) cooking apples
3oz (84g) sugar (approx)
Water
Butter
Half a dozen slices of day old, or older, bread
1tbsp golden syrup
2tbsp hot water

Peel, core and slice the apples, and simmer in water with
sugar to taste until soft. Butter a pudding basin and line with
slices of stale bread. Spoon in one-third of the apple pulp,
cover with a slice of bread, and continue to layer the apple
and bread until all the apple is used, finishing with bread.
Mix the syrup and hot water and pour over the pudding.
Cover with a saucer and weight it down. Leave overnight
before turning out. Serve with syrup and whipped cream.

WARWICKSHIRE

Chitterlings

Chitterlings are, to be blunt, the intestines of a slaughtered
animal, invariably those of a pig. They seem to be associated
with Warwickshire for some unknown reason, although
Lincolnshire does have its Pig's Fry, but they are not very
much in favour today. They are occasionally sold already
cooked, jellied and pressed like tongue, in delicatessens, and
are pleasant enough to eat. After all we are not worried that
many ordinary butchers' sausages are encased in skins made
from animal innards.

WELLINGBOROUGH

I found myself in Wellingborough in Northamptonshire on
an early-closing afternoon, but as luck would have it, one
butcher-cum-fish shop was still open. The owner, dressed
in one of those natty striped rigouts, admitted he was a
great fan of Hock and Dough, and confirmed that the old
recipe still reigned supreme in Wellingborough kitchens. In
fact, on more than one occasion, the name of the dish has
been used in place of the town's proper name on mail, and
local postmen have had to contend with . . . Road, Hock and
Dough, Northants.

The local football team is known as 'The Doughboys', which makes them a fine (if flabby with all that doughy stodge) match for 'The Leeks' who play at nearby Earl's Barton.

The following jingle appeared in *This England*, Winter 1974.

> Six a song of sixpence,
> A pan of 'Ock 'n Dough'
> Put four 'n twenty taters
> A stannin' in a row;
> When the Ock is added an'
> The Dough set in a ring
> Aroun' the pan, see there me man
> A dish fit furra king!
>
> But dawn't furget the onions,
> The pepper 'n the salt,
> An' cook it very slow, like,
> Aw you s'll be at fault;
> Serve it up wi' Brussel Knobs,
> Brockerlie or kale,
> If you should wish a scrumshuss dish
> The Ock'll no ways fail!

Wellingborough Hock (or Hough) and Dough

Pork hock joint about 1½lb (675g)
2oz (56g) lard
4oz (112g) plain flour
Pinch salt
2oz (56g) shredded suet
2 or 3 large potatoes, peeled and sliced
2 onions, skinned and sliced
1tsp sage
Salt and pepper
Hot stock or water

Rub the fat into the flour and salt to make a breadcrumb-like mixture, and stir in the shredded suet. Add enough cold water to make a soft, but not sticky dough. Turn onto a floured board and roll out. Cut suitable lengths to line the sides (not base) of your meat tin. Put the hock in the centre of the tin, and surround it with the sliced potatoes and onions. Sprinkle with sage, salt and pepper. Pour in sufficient hot stock to half fill the tin and cover the whole lot with foil. Place in an oven preheated to 400°F (200°C; Gas mark 6). After 10–15min, when the liquid should be on the point of boiling, lower the oven temperature a few degrees, or a mark, so that a simmer is maintained. Cook for 1½hr and then remove foil. Return to the oven for another ½hr to brown. The cooking times may vary according to the size and shape of the meat tin, and of course a larger hock will take a little longer.

WENSLEYDALE

Cheese

Wensleydale in the old North Riding of Yorkshire is a fertile and prosperous valley that has given its name to a rather delicate cheese. The blue-veined variety is believed to have been introduced by the Normans. Then monks, who inhabited Yorkshire's Jervaulx Abbey from the late twelfth century onwards, somehow obtained the recipe. They continued to make Wensleydale Cheese, quite successfully, until the dissolution of the monastery. The Abbey is now in ruins and the cheese is mostly made in creameries, with the exception of a few farmers who still practise the old crafts. Nowadays there are two varieties – the white Wensleydale which is mild and flaky with a slight tang, and the old, rich, blue-veined Wensleydale which is not seen so frequently these days. The white variety goes well with apple pie.

Nodden cakes are not really cakes at all but little pastry biscuits. They were always well buttered, and were a favourite snack with field workers at hay-making time.

Wensleydale Nodden Cakes

8oz (225g) plain flour
Pinch salt
4oz (112g) butter or lard
Water

Sift the flour and salt and rub in the butter or lard. Mix to a pastry with water and roll out fairly thinly. Cut into any shapes, plain or fancy, and bake on an oiled tray at 425°F (220°C; Gas mark 7) for 15min, until crispy and brown.

In other parts of Yorkshire, Sad Cakes was another name for these plain little things.

WESTMORLAND

The old county of Westmorland – now married off with Cumberland as Cumbria – is renowned for its Tatie Pot. It is a hot, filling stew which is made locally with Herdwick lamb, a breed of rather funny looking sheep peculiar to this county. Originally these sheep were bred for their wool which was considered to be especially hard wearing and suitable for carpets. This wool was traded in the West Indies and the Far East for brown sugar, rum and spices, and it was the illicit smuggling of these imports that led to the carefree use of costly ingredients like rum in the recipes of poor country folk (see Cumberland section). Tatie Pot was once sold in Westmorland pubs in large stew jars, and Tatie Pot Suppers were regular events.

Westmorland Tatie Pot   (Serves 4–6)

1½lb (675g) stewing lamb
2 large onions
2 carrots
1lb (450g) black pudding
1½lb (675g) potatoes
Salt and pepper
1 pint (560ml) hot stock (approx)
Dripping

Trim the lamb and cut into pieces. Skin and slice the onions, and chop up the carrots and black pudding into rounds. Peel and slice the potatoes. Layer all these ingredients in a casserole, seasoning with salt and pepper as you go, and finish with some potatoes on top. Pour in the hot stock to within ½in of the top and brush the top potatoes with a little dripping. Put in an oven preheated to 400°F (200°C; Gas mark 6) for 1½–2hr. To encourage the potatoes to brown, they can be brushed with more dripping midway through the cooking.

Tatie Pot is always accompanied by Pickled Red Cabbage.

Pickled Red Cabbage

1 firm red cabbage – about 2½lb (1.125kg)
Cooking salt
1½ pints (840ml) white malt vinegar (approx)
1 good tbsp pickling spices

Discard the tough outer leaves and stalky bits of the cabbage. Wash and shred it, and layer in a large china bowl sprinkling each layer with plenty of salt. Leave overnight and rinse off all the salt by running water through it in a colander. Pack into jars. Simmer the vinegar and spices together for an hour and strain. When cool – this is important or else you will cook the cabbage – pour over the cabbage. Cover and store for about a week before using, but do not keep for longer than three months as it tends to lose its crunchiness.

The recipe below is for an old Westmorland Herb Pudding that used to be made in the spring when green vegetables were scarce. It was claimed, like the Calder Valley Dock Pudding, to be a spring medicine and very good for the system. The leaves were gathered from the hedgerows in large bowls, by country folk. Spinach can be substituted when easterledge is not available, and a few dandelion leaves can be thrown in as well.

Westmorland Easterledge Pudding

1 large bowl of easterledge and young nettle tops
4oz (112g) pearl barley
Salt and pepper
2oz (56g) butter

Wash the greenery, discarding the stalks and any tough bits. Chop up finely and mix with the pearl barley. Put in a muslin bag and boil for 2hr. Turn into a warm dish. Season to taste and fork in the butter. Serve immediately as a hot vegetable.

WILTSHIRE

Today, along with most other things, the price of a loaf of bread seems to be forever rising, but this was not always the case. In 1800 a gallon of corn for bread cost 3s 4d (17p) and this price actually fell to a mere 10d (4p) in 1904. (There is hope for us yet.) The corn information is inscribed on stone tablets on a wall by St Giles Church in Great Wishford, Wiltshire. These tablets were erected in 1965 to replace the original ones which had deteriorated badly, and show the variations in bread prices from the year 1800 to the present day.

Another bready Wiltshire curiosity is the tale of the Swindon sandwich. It concerns the building of the Great Western Railway that helped to turn Swindon into a prosperous industrial town. A railway engineer, Daniel Gooch, drew up the plans for the proposed railway and, in 1833, they were approved by another engineer named Brugel. However, according to legend, the two men could not decide exactly where to start the building operations, and so sat on Swindon's furze covered hillside to contemplate the problem over their sandwich lunches. It was then agreed that a sandwich should be thrown, and that the building would be commenced wherever it landed.

For all its bready folklore, Wiltshire has no outstanding bread recipe. There is, however, the famous Wiltshire Lardy Cake, which is still popular in the county and imitated by many bakers throughout Britain.

Wiltshire Lardy Cake

½oz (14g) fresh yeast
1 level tsp sugar
¼ pint (140ml) warm (hand hot) water
8oz (225g) strong, plain white flour
1 level tsp salt
3oz (84g) lard
1 level tsp mixed spice
2oz (56g) sugar
2oz (56g) dried fruit
1 level tbsp golden syrup

Sift the flour and salt together and rub in 1oz (28g) of the lard. Mix the fresh yeast with one teaspoon of sugar in the warm water and pour into the sifted ingredients. Knead for a few minutes. Cover with an oiled polythene sheet and put in a warmish place until it doubles in bulk. Turn out onto a floured board and roll out to an oblong about ¼in thick. Dab on 1oz of the remaining lard and sprinkle on half of the spice, half the sugar, and half the dried fruit. Fold in 3, turn to left (as in flaky pastry making) and roll out again. Dab on last 1oz lard, and sprinkle on remaining spice, sugar and dried fruit. Fold in 3 again, and roll out to an oblong about 1in thick. Put in a greased, oblong meat tin and make diagonal scores across the top. Cover with an oiled polythene sheet and leave to prove again. Bake in an oven preheated to 400°F (200°C; Gas mark 6) for about 35min. Brush the top with golden syrup and leave to cool on a wire rack.

Another Wiltshire recipe is for Porkie Sausages. These are sausage meatballs, fried in batter and served with apple rings.

Wiltshire Porkies

2 large cooking apples
4oz (112g) flour
Pinch salt
1 egg, separated
2tsp cooking oil
¼ pint (140ml) milk and water
1lb (450g) sausagemeat
Oil for deep-frying

Peel, core and slice the apples into rings. Sieve the flour and salt and mix in the yolk, cooking oil, milk and water. Roll the sausagemeat into balls. When you are ready to fry, whisk the egg white and fold into the batter. Coat the sausage meatballs with batter and deep fry in hot oil for about 12min. Drain and keep warm. Coat the apple rings with batter and deep fry for 4–5min. Drain and serve immediately with the porkies.

Tracklements

Wiltshire Tracklements are old-fashioned meat accompaniments. Some are based on apple jellies and flavoured with thyme or sage, others are spiced jellies, or mustards (see Urchfont section).

WINDSOR

Windsor in Berkshire is dominated by its famous castle, which is the largest inhabited castle in the world. Edward III was responsible for founding the Order of the Knights of the Garter, thus making Windsor a centre for chivalry, but I cannot put forth any theory as to why this dish is known as Poor Knights of Windsor.

Poor Knights of Windsor

¼ pint (140ml) white wine (or milk)
2 rounded tbsp brown sugar
1 level tsp cinnamon
Several slices white bread
2 egg yolks
Butter for frying
Strawberry jam

Mix the white wine with the sugar and cinnamon in a shallow dish. In another similar dish, fork-mix the egg yolks. Take one or two slices of bread, depending on the size of your frying pan, and dip both sides in the sweet spiced wine and then in the egg yolk. Fry in hot melted butter until golden brown on both sides. Keep warm while you fry the other slices. Serve immediately spread lavishly with strawberry jam.

Red Cheese

Windsor Red Cheese is a unique and original cheese which is distributed by Charles Liles & Son. It is produced for them in a Midland dairy and is an harmonious blend of cheese and wine – basically a mild Cheddar with Elderberry wine. Many 'wine' cheeses have been produced through the years but this attempt, first made in the late 1960s, seems to be one of the most successful to date.

WORCESTERSHIRE

Worcestershire Sauce

The legend of Worcestershire Sauce is entertaining and yet quite credible. The story begins in 1823 when a druggist, Mr John Wheeley Lea, and a chemist, Mr William Perrins, pooled their knowledge and became partners in Mr Lea's drug store at 68, Broad Street, Worcester.

In 1835, they were asked by a Worcestershire nobleman, Lord Sandys, who had recently returned from the East, to make up a recipe he had acquired in India. Mr Lea and Mr Perrins did just that, and in addition to Lord Sandys' order, they made a few barrels for their own use. However, when they tasted it, they thought it so horrible, they left the barrels at the back of the cellar. Time passed and eventually the sauce was remembered and destined to be thrown out. Out of curiosity, they tasted the brew once again, and found to the amazement that it had matured to a superlative sauce.

Thus Lea and Perrins have been making 'the original and genuine Worcestershire Sauce' since 1837 to the same old

Indian recipe. The formula and process are secret but it is made by extracting the flavours from various fruits, vegetables, anchovies, spices and other ingredients, by placing them in vinegar in wooden barrels, for a long period of time without using heat. Its piquant flavour is unique and no cook would be without it, though it can also be used as a table sauce.

Alas, Messrs Lea and Perrins' little shop at 68, Broad Street is now a building society, but Worcestershire Sauce will, I am sure, be regarded as one of Britain's great culinary assets for many centuries to come.

It was while I was traipsing round the streets of Worcester in search of the old Lea and Perrins establishment that I happened to spot an unusual biscuit in a baker's shop window; a round shortbread type with nuts. An assistant told me that they were known as sables. I wrote to Cadena Cakes, owners of the shop, and caused quite a stir as the directors in Bristol were not familiar with the name sable, and it could not be traced. It was finally established that the biscuit was officially known as 'Parisienne Platten', and had been introduced by the firm in 1948, following one of their executive's annual visits to France.

Somehow 'Parisienne Platten' does not sound as if it fits in this book, but it *was* on sale, round and bold in Worcester. So for want of a better name, here is my recipe for Worcester Sables.

Worcester Sables   (Makes 8 or 9)

3oz (84g) butter
3oz (84g) caster sugar
1 egg yolk
6oz (168g) plain flour
Pinch salt
Milk
2oz (56g) shelled hazelnuts

Lightly grease a large baking sheet. Cream the butter and 2½oz (70g) of the sugar together until light and fluffy; beat in the egg yolk. Sift the flour with the salt, and mix into the creamed mixture, with the nuts and as much milk as needed to make a soft dough. Cover and put in the refrigerator for an hour or so, to become firm. Turn onto a lightly floured board and roll out as thin as the nuts will allow. Using a 3in cutter, cut rounds and put on prepared sheet. Brush with milk and sprinkle with remaining sugar. Bake in an oven preheated to 400°F (200°C; Gas mark 6) for about 25min, until golden.

YORK

York, the capital of Yorkshire, is neatly encircled by 2½ miles of medieval wall, much of which is still intact, and dates from the thirteenth century. Within these maternal walls is a web of historic streets, winding here, there, and everywhere, and a famous one is aptly named 'The Shambles'.

Ham

York's most obvious glory is the imposing Minster with its wealth of medieval stained glass. According to legend, it was the Minster's construction that led to one of England's most famous recipes – York Ham. The oak trees that were used to build the Minster were sawn on site, and the sawdust was found to be ideal for smoking local hams. A traditional York Ham is much larger than a normal ham, and can weigh up to 50lb. It is a dry, salted ham cured with salt-petre and left to hang for a whole year. This results in excellent keeping qualities as opposed to those of ordinary hams which only keep fresh for several weeks following their short steeping time in brine. Unfortunately York Hams are not economical to produce today and are rarely found outside York. Scotts in York's Petergate still advertise local hams, and many Yorkshire pig farmers still cure their hams in December for the following year's Christmas.

Chocolate

Besides the Minster, visitors to York flock to the Castle Museum which includes an authentic reconstruction of an eighteenth-century shopping village. In Princess Mary Court there is a particularly fascinating sweet shop named Joseph

Terry & Sons. A shop such as this started trading lozenges, comfits and candied peel in 1767, and the business blossomed into the now famous Terry's of York – noted throughout the world as confectioners and perhaps most of all for their chocolate products. However, it is seldom realised that chocolate as we know it today was not invented until the mid-nineteenth century: up until that period chocolate was a drink, and was spelt 'jocalette' by the diarist, Samuel Pepys. George Bernard Shaw (1856–1950) asked: 'What use are cartridges in battle? I always carry chocolate instead. (*Arms and the Man*)

YORKSHIRE

Yorkshire's most famous food is probably the batter puddings which accompany England's traditional Sunday roast beef. Yorkshire Pudding is an age-old recipe which every Yorkshire housewife has her own perfect way of making. Although normally associated with roast beef, 'Yorkshires', as the individual puddings are commonly known, can be served with any roast meat. Today we usually serve them with the main course but in some parts of Yorkshire, they still follow the old tradition of eating them before the main course, smothered in thick gravy. This dish was called the 'sheet anchor' of a Yorkshireman's dinner. In some parts of the country, the pudding was, and occasionally still is, dished up as afters, sweetened with jam, sauce, syrup or sugar. The puddings, both large and small, were invariably baked in dripping pans placed under the joint roasting in front of the fire, so that the dripping from the joint flavoured the batter handsomely.

Yorkshire Pudding (Serves 6)

4oz (112g) plain flour
Pinch of salt
2 eggs
½ pint (280ml) milk and water mixed (approx)
Little dripping

Sieve the flour and salt into a bowl and make a well in the centre. Add the eggs and beat well. Pour in enough milk and water to make a smooth pouring batter, and beat again until bubbles appear. Ideally, cover the bowl and leave for 1hr before using, but the result will still be edible if you skip this stage. Pour a little dripping into one large tin, or several individual tins if preferred, and warm for 5min in the oven. Pour in the batter and bake for 15–20min, depending on size, in an oven preheated to about 425°F (220°C; Gas mark 7).

Not far behind the celebrated Yorkshire Pudding in popularity is Parkin, a gingerbread speciality which is acclaimed far and near. This is not a dainty delicacy but more rugged, like the Yorkshire countryside, and dark and spicy. It keeps very well and this had led to the Yorkshire saying, to one who is ill, 'Don't worry – you'll soon be like a parkin'. In Yorkshire it is often made for Guy Fawkes night to accompany the blazing and sparkling extravaganza. Incidentally, the legendary Guy Fawkes was born in Yorkshire, in the vicinity of York Minster.

Yorkshire Parkin

8oz (225g) wholemeal flour
Generous pinch of salt
2 level tsp ground ginger
1 level tsp mace
1 level tsp nutmeg
6oz (168g) medium oatmeal
1oz (28g) brown sugar
4oz (112g) dark treacle
4oz (112g) golden syrup
2oz (56g) margarine
8 fluid oz (225ml) warm milk
2 level tsp bicarbonate of soda
1 egg

Mix the flour, salt and spices thoroughly in a bowl. Stir in the oatmeal and the sugar. Weigh the treacle and syrup into a saucepan. This is done more easily if you stand the pan and spoon on the scales and calculate accordingly. Add the margarine and put the saucepan on a low heat. Stir until the margarine melts. Dissolve the bicarbonate of soda in the warm (hand-hot) milk and add with the treacle, syrup and melted margarine and lightly beaten egg to the dry ingredients. Mix to make a sloppy, almost batter-like mixture, and pour into a greased meat tin about 10in × 8in. Bake in an oven preheated to 325°F (170°C; Gas mark 3) for 40min. Leave to cool on a wire rack. Parkin is best left in a tin for a few days before eating. A popular Yorkshire custom is to serve wedges of Parkin topped with stewed apple.

Yorkshire Teacakes are large, round and curranty, and are good toasted, split and buttered for tea.

Yorkshire Teacakes   (Makes about 8)

YEAST LIQUID
1oz (28g) fresh yeast
1 tsp sugar
¼ pint (140ml) warm water
DOUGH
1lb (450g) plain flour
1 level tsp salt
1oz (28g) butter
2oz (56g) currants
1oz (28g) sugar
¼ pint (140ml) warm milk
Milk for glaze

Cream the fresh yeast with a teaspoonful of sugar and the warm water. Sieve the flour and salt, and rub in the butter. Stir in the currants, sugar, warm milk and yeast liquid, and mix to make a softish dough. Turn onto a floured board and knead until smooth. Put in a bowl, cover with an oiled polythene sheet and leave in a warm place to double in size. Turn onto board again, knead a bit, and break into 8 equal pieces. Roll each piece into a flat round. Place on a lightly greased baking tray – do not crowd them – remember they will spread when baked. Leave to prove again for about 15min and then brush them with milk. Bake in a preheated oven at 425°F (220°C; Gas mark 7) for about 15min, when they should be golden brown.

Similar to teacakes, but not made with yeast, are Fat Rascals, or Turf Cakes as they were known on the moors where they were cooked in the open on a griddle over a turf fire.

Fat Rascals or Turf Cakes

4oz (112g) lard or butter
8oz (225g) self-raising flour
Good pinch of salt
3oz (84g) sugar
2oz (56g) currants
2oz (56g) sultanas
Water
Milk

Rub the lard or butter into the flour and salt. Add the other ingredients using enough water to make a fairly soft dough. Roll out on a floured board to about ½in thick. Cut rounds and brush with milk. Bake on a greased tray at 425°F (220°C; Gas mark 7) for 15min.

Caraway seeds were once more popular than they are today. The plants were often grown in country gardens; the leaves were eaten like lettuce and the seeds used to flavour cheese and cakes amongst other things. Seed Cakes were once especially favoured in Yorkshire and there are numerous recipes for them ranging from the very plain to the exceedingly rich. The number of caraway seeds that you stir in is a matter of how 'seedy' you like your cake. Caraway essence is sometimes substituted when seeds are unavailable.

Yorkshire Seed Cake

8oz (225g) self-raising flour
½ level tsp salt
4oz (112g) butter
4oz (112g) sugar
1–3oz (28–84g) caraway seeds
2 eggs, beaten
½ cup milk (approx)

Grease and line a 7in cake tin. Mix the flour and salt, and rub in the butter until the mixture resembles breadcrumbs. Stir in the sugar and seeds. Make a well in the middle and add the beaten eggs and enough milk to make a mixture of dropping consistency. Turn into prepared tin and bake at 350°F (180°C; Gas mark 4) for 1hr. The cake should be golden brown and firm to touch. It is not iced as it is traditionally eaten plain.

Seed cakes were very popular at the end of sowing time when the menfolk returned home at dusk, exhausted and hungry.

> Wife, some time this week, if the weather hold clear,
> An end of wheat sowing we make for this year:
> Remember thou therefore, though I do it not,
> The seed-cake, the pasties, and the furmenty pot.
> (Thomas Tusser, 1573)

ACKNOWLEDGEMENTS

The author wishes to thank the following individuals and organisations for their generous assistance in compiling this book:

Anglesey Area Library; His Grace The Duke of Atholl; Town Clerk, Aylesbury; Clerk and Chief Officer, Bakewell; *Banbury Guardian* (1884); Barker & Dobson; Mrs H. C. Barnet ALA, Bury Public Library; Mrs Jane Barrows, Librarian, Market Harborough; L. T. and A. J. R. Bates, Kentish Vineyards; Sylvia Bell; Blackburn Information Bureau; Christine Bloxham, Banbury Library and Museum; C. M. Bondfield, Publicity Officer, Southend-on-Sea; A. W. Bridges FLA, Central Library, Great Yarmouth; Mrs A. Bromley; Theo Brown, Hon Research Fellow in British Folklore, Exeter; H. P. Bulmer Ltd; James Burrough Ltd; Town Clerk, Burton-on-Trent; Cadbury Schweppes Ltd; Cadena Cakes Ltd; Kenneth R. Cann, Grantham; Carlisle Public Library; Catlin Bros Ltd; Town Clerk, Chorley; Coates & Co (Plymouth) Ltd; Colchester Oyster Fishery Ltd; Mrs Joyce Conyingham Green; Cornish Mead Co Ltd; Coronation Rock Co Ltd; Coventry Information Centre; John Curtis, Isle of Man; Devon County Council; Dundee Library; The Dunmow Flitch Bacon Company; Dunmow Rural District Council; Edinburgh Central Library; C. Edwards, Chelsea Library; John Farrah, Harrogate; Felixstowe Town Hall; Alex Ferguson Ltd; Folkestone Public Library; Peter Foster; Mrs Gardiner, Market Harborough; Gloucestershire County Library; Goldencap Biscuit Bakery; R. Goodbody Esq; Arthur Guinness Son and Co Ltd; Mrs Betty Hardy; Town Clerk, Harrogate; John Harvey & Sons Ltd; A. A. C. Hedges FLA, Great Yarmouth Public Library; Hereford Town Hall; S. C. Holliday, Chelsea Library; Mr L. V. Homewood JP; J. P. Hopwood, Priston Mill Farm; Huntley & Palmers; Vivien Igoe, Irish Tourist Board; Irish Mist Liqueur Co Ltd; Royal Jersey Agricultural & Horticultural Society; Jersey Department of Agriculture; Jersey Local History Librarian; James Keiller & Son Ltd; Kendal Town Hall; K. E. Kissack, Hon Director, Monmouth Museum; Mr W. H. Lambert; Lawson of Dyce Ltd; Mr C. P. Le Cornu, Jersey; Mrs Kathleen Lee; Leicester Library; Charles Liles & Son; Lowestoft and East Suffolk Maritime Society; Lowestoft Central Library; Maldon Crystal Salt Co Ltd; Paul H. Manning; R. E. Marston FLA, Derby Central Library; Mr and Mrs Martell, Laurel Farm; Melton Mowbray Urban District Council; Mrs A. Merrell; Merrydown Wine Company Ltd; E. G. Millard Esq, Cheddar; Mrs D. J.

Morris; P. J. Newens, Newens & Sons Ltd; North West Tourist Board; Nottingham Central Library; J. W. Nunn, Spa Director, Bath; Mr and Mrs Michael O'Mara, The Bacon Company of Ireland Ltd; Park Cake Bakeries Ltd; Parker-Bradburn Ltd; S. Parkinson & Son (Doncaster) Ltd; John Peet; Kathleen B. Pike; Edgar Purton; Daniel Quiggin & Son, Kendal; Reckitt & Colman, Norwich; Mr K. Rennison, Dunnington, York; London Borough of Richmond upon Thames; Town Clerk, Ripon; L. Robson & Sons Ltd; Mrs Anne Rogan; Rowntree Mackintosh Ltd; Norman A. Rudd, Huntingdon; Rutland Arms Hotel, Bakewell; Vicar of St Briavel's Church; Major-General Sir Guy Salisbury-Jones GCVO, CMG, CBE, MC; Scottish Tourist Board; Shrewsbury Information Bureau; Standard Group of Newspapers; Kathleen Stephenson; The Stilton Cheese Makers Association; Swindon Central Library; Alfred Taylor (Bath) Ltd; Joseph Terry & Sons Ltd; Rev F. H. J. Thomas; Ingram Thompson & Sons Ltd; Alfreda Thompson; Catering Manager, Trinity College, Cambridge; Gordon Trueman, Lea & Perrins Ltd; Helen Tullberg, Wiltshire Tracklement Co Ltd; Tunbridge Wells Town Hall; United Biscuits Ltd; Mrs Alice J. Waller; Bill and Sam Ward, Manchester; Watty Foods Ltd; Welsh Tourist Board; The Western Morning News Co Ltd; Whitbread & Co Ltd; Wilkin & Son Ltd, Tiptree; Margaret Willis, Charles Cotton Hotel, Derbyshire; A. Wilson, Coventry Reference Library; Mrs Margaret G. Wilson; Mrs Joyce Withers; Mr Young, Ye Olde Pork Pie Shoppe, Melton Mowbray; Yorkshire Biscuits Ltd; *Yorkshire Evening Post*.

In addition, the author thanks the following for kind permission to reproduce copyright material:

Jonathan Cape Ltd for excerpts from *Good Things in England* by Florence White used in the Eccles and London sections (this book is now also available as a paperback from Futura Books); *Daily Mail* for material from an article by Vincent Mulchrone used in the London section; Sheila Hutchins for material from *Your Granny's Cookbook* published by Daily Express Publications (1971) and *English Recipes and Others* published by Methuen & Co Ltd (1967) used in the London and Welsh sections; The Folklore Society for extracts from *British Calendar Customs*, used in various sections; Paul Jennings for extract from *Even Oddier* used in Dundee section; Jersey WI for material from *Buon Appetit* used in the Jersey section; New English Library and Merrydown Wine Company for material from *The Merrydown Book of Country Wines* by André Launay (1968) used in the Sussex section; Oxford University Press for